Educating for Wisdom in the 21st Century

Other Books of Interest from St. Augustine's Press

Richard Bishirjian, *The Coming Death and Future Resurrection of American Higher Education: 1885–2017*

James V. Schall, *Docilitas: On Teaching and Being Taught*

Harold Henderson, *Let's Kill Dick and Jane: How the Open Court Publishing Company Fought the Culture of American Education*

Friedrich Nietzsche, *On the Future of Our Educational Institutions*

H. S. Gerdil, *The Anti-Emile: Reflections on the Theory and Practice of Education against the Principles of Rousseau*

Barry G. Hankins and Donald D. Schmeltekopf, *The Baylor Project: Taking Christian Higher Education to the Next Level*

Michael Davis, *Wonderlust: Ruminations on Liberal Education*

Charles E. Rice, *What Happened to Notre Dame?*

Thomas Aquinas, *Treatise on Law: The Complete Text*

Peter Augustine Lawler, *Homeless and at Home in America*

Peter Augustine Lawler, *American Heresies and Higher Education*

Roger Scruton, *The Aesthetic Understanding: Essays in the Philosophy of Art and Culture*

Roger Scruton, *An Intelligent Person's Guide to Modern Culture*

Roger Kimball, *The Fortunes of Permanence: Culture and Anarchy in an Age of Amnesia*

Frederic Raphael and Joseph Epstein, *Where Were We?*

Peter Kreeft, *Summa Philosophica*

Peter Kreeft, *The Sea Within*

Josef Pieper, *What Does "Academic" Mean?: Two Essays on the Chances of the University Today*

Josef Pieper, *Enthusiasm and Divine Madness*

Josef Pieper, *Don't Worry about Socrates*

Educating for Wisdom
in the 21st Century

Darin H. Davis, Editor

St. Augustine's Press
South Bend, Indiana

Manufactured in the United States of America.

1 2 3 4 5 6   25 24 23 22 21 20 19

Library of Congress Control Number: 2016944267

∞ The paper used in this publication meets the minimum
requirements of the American National Standard for Information Sciences -
Permanence of Paper for Printed Materials, ANSI Z39.48-1984.

St. Augustine's Press
www.staugustine.net

Table of Contents

Foreword

"Where can wisdom be found? And where is the place of understanding?"
(Job 28:12)

Coincident with what, for half a century now, has been variously referred to as "the crisis in higher education," there has been a less widely noticed atrophy of wisdom as a subject for academic reflection, let alone as one imagined outcome of a good university education. Various explanations for this demise have been offered: technological revolution, the evident economic advantages of narrower professional school training, and the now exclusive dominion of science as the standard and arbiter of value in education are among them. Concern for the demise of wisdom has recently been expressed by prominent humanist educators, including some of the contributors to this volume. Others, also represented here, have expressed resignation about the inevitable decline of wisdom as a conceivable goal of contemporary education, given the priorities of the research university. Only rarely have these divergent points of view been brought together in such a useful conversation as we find here.

The conversation is necessary in my view, if for no other reason than that the crisis in the university mirrors an identity crisis in the wider culture. Are the goals our culture most values the acquisition of personal wealth, the advancement of technologies to control our environment, and entertainments to provide therapy for our disappointments? Perhaps unsurprisingly, over the last half-century these have been increasingly the incentives that have shaped university education as well. As will be obvious to anyone who follows our media oracles for what counts as newsworthy, short-term success in achieving these goals—in particular material success—has become our cultural First Principle. Equally apparent is that it requires little in the way of wisdom to achieve this kind of success—at least in the short-term.

If our founding universities in Europe in the high Middle Ages had a different orientation to the purposes of a university education, it was because they had a different First Principle, now seen by many as outmoded. Rather than short-term success, thinkers such as Thomas Aquinas and Bonaventure sought an integration of all knowledge with a concept of timeless Wisdom, a wisdom that endures because its source is in eternal truths. Thus Aquinas distinguished between someone who has merely acquired a body of knowledge and one who has obtained a perspective that relates it and other branches of knowledge to a higher principle:

> A wise man in any branch of knowledge is one who knows the highest cause of that knowledge, and is able to judge of all matters by that cause; and a wise man absolutely is one who knows that cause which is absolutely highest, namely God. Hence, the knowledge of eternal things is called wisdom, while the knowledge of human things is called knowledge. (ST 2.2a.q.2)

In this view, both Aristotelian and biblical, our present university curricula must be judged as providing well-advanced opportunities for the acquisition of knowledge—various components of what Aquinas called scientia. As for the possibility of higher causes—whether according to Aristotle or as characterized in Christian theology—the reality of what Aquinas called wisdom (*sapientia*) is not on the menu. Most of our students have had scant opportunity even to consider whether such a quality of cognition might exist.

Wisdom, after all, is not simple. Very early in the pages which follow we are reminded that, for Aristotle, there were two branches of wisdom: theoretical and practical (*sophia* and *phronesis*, respectively). Both branches he thought necessary and complementary, even mutually indispensable. Such a relation (with important nuances) is observable at the semantic level in languages other than Greek and Latin. In Hebrew, for example, *chokma* is a quality of synthetic wisdom, the highest form of which is the wisdom of God that created the world (Prov. 8:22–30); *binah*, discernment or understanding, is the practical wisdom necessary to contemplate it, while *da'at*, ordinary knowledge, is a matter of data and tertiary. In Chinese, similar distinctions pertain; the word for wisdom, *zhi hui*, has two characters 智慧, the first signifying a theoretical and changeless element, the second a practical dimension of intellectual acuity. In our time, however, globalized education—having first divorced the two "wisdom" elements from each other—has abandoned both for an obsessive preoccupation with the gathering and packaging of information. The result is we have produced a form of higher education that does quite well by way of transmitting knowledge and information, but much less well by way of guiding personal formation, and very poorly at providing opportunities for intellectual or spiritual transformation. The secular reflections that begin this book and the more theologically attuned essays that conclude it are all keenly aware of this circumstance, and seek to address it. The essay by editor and co-author Darin Davis reaches in both directions, fully cognizant of the fact that in our fragmented era no univocal advocacy can produce much progress in redressing the loss of balance that has resulted from our neglect of wisdom.

It is a commendation of the integrity of this volume that none of the contributors fancies that there is anything like a quick fix to an imbalance so long in the making. Descartes, the Renaissance philosopher from whom so much of modern educational method is derived, was prophetic of our partiality with his dictum that "the sciences altogether are identical with human wisdom."[1] What this means, of course, is that even learned individuals cannot hope ever to know enough to possess wisdom; in fact, as the hypertrophy and balkanization of contemporary academic disciplines make clear, neither, according to such a definition, can the collectivity of the university. Implicit in such early modern views—including the

---

1   René Descartes, *Rules for the Direction of the Mind*, vol. 1 of *The Philosophical Works of Descartes*, trans. Elizabeth S. Haldane and G. R. T. Ross (Cambridge: Cambridge University Press, 1967), 1.

contention of Francis Bacon that only up-to-date scientific knowledge counts as real learning—is a rejection of the wisdom of the past and its concern for metaphysics and moral enquiry in favor of present, more material preoccupations. Accordingly, one diagnostic question to test what might be counted as worthy of higher education might be put in this way: "Can anything of the past be a relevant authority for us today?" The question is diagnostic simply because those who have made short-term success their First Principle will generally, consciously or unconsciously, already have answered in the negative. Those who take a longer view, and whose idea of educational success is not measured exclusively in materialistic terms, are likely to believe that ideas and beliefs from the past need to have a measure of authority today if we are not to lose an immense amount of indispensable cultural capital. Wisdom is, after all, by definition the product of intellectual and spiritual accrual, in cultures as well as in individuals.

Few who come to this important little book will be unaware of the uncertainty and lack of conviction concerning the future of the university its authors seek to address. For a disabling length of time, the "conventional wisdom" of higher education theory and practice has privileged form and fashion over content and ends, social convention over intellectual curiosity; and, regarding student achievement, immediate self-esteem over a lifetime appreciation of personal fulfillment. Whatever our gains, mounting losses now threaten those gains. A question which I think every reader of *Educating for Wisdom in the 21st Century University* is bound to ask is whether our tangible goods, bereft of any relationship to a higher intelligible Good, may not prove to be ephemeral. On our collective willingness to come together to wrestle with that question, I submit, depends the future of the university, and perhaps of our culture more generally.

David Lyle Jeffrey

Introduction
Darin H. Davis

Historian Hastings Rashdall once described the universities of medieval Europe—schools founded by the Church in places like Paris
and Bologna—as committed to the "consecration of learning."[1]
Rigorous and comprehensive in their program of learning (students
pursued arithmetic, geometry, astronomy, music theory, grammar,
logic, and rhetoric as well as moral philosophy, physics, and metaphysics), medieval universities were strikingly different than their
twenty-first century descendants. They had no research labs, athletic facilities, or career placement centers. There were no student
life programs, no social or service organizations. Their leaders did
not have to concern themselves with boards of trustees, alumni
groups, or accreditation agencies. There were no multi-million dol-
lar development campaigns. Instead, what defined these first universities was their commitment to a broad, intensive program of
teaching and learning that served the purposes of moral, intellectual, and spiritual formation. Universities were not expansive campuses with well-equipped classrooms, but communities of teachers
and students pursuing wisdom in the light of the Divine.

In our day, the mission statements and curricula of many small,
private liberal arts colleges and even large state-supported universities still express various of these same commitments to teaching
and learning, though not always in a manner that is theologically
inspired. "Higher learning," in the truest and best sense of the expression, continues in the twenty-first century, but it is by no means

1   Hastings Rashdall, *The Universities in Europe in the Middle* Ages, 3
    vols. (Oxford: Oxford University Press, 1936) III, 442.

the defining mark of contemporary higher education. Universities now are expected to advance highly specialized research across the academic disciplines. Universities likewise are charged with the task of preparing and credentialing students for the workforce, so much so that career preparation and placement are for many the university's *summum bonum*. Pursuing truth, knowledge, and virtue still sound like perfectly laudable pursuits, but they are not the first things—or even the second things—that define the life of the university.

The contributors to this volume contend that the essential task of the modern academy should be seeking, teaching, and cultivating wisdom. They do not merely lament the current state of higher education, nor do they wax nostalgic for bygone days. They do seek, however, to understand more precisely the reason why educating for wisdom is so difficult today. Furthermore, they seek to understand more clearly what wisdom is, where it may be found, and how it again might animate teaching and learning in the university.

The volume begins with contributions by Anthony Kronman and Andrew Delbanco, both of whom have written insightful works on contemporary higher education.[2] Kronman's essay, "Wisdom in the Age of the Research Ideal," asks whether the pursuit of wisdom is even possible today given the modern academy's research ambitions. Drawing on Aristotle's distinction between theoretical and practical wisdom, Kronman argues that the Greek conception of wisdom assumes, on one hand, that theoretical wisdom can at least in principle be perfected, and that practical wisdom cannot be taught. But the Abrahamic doctrine of creation effectively dissolves the distinction between form and matter that the Aristotelian conception of wisdom depends upon. The world is now *infinitely* intelligible; indeed, no one can ever (in principle or reality) know everything that can be known about the world. Accordingly,

---

2   Andrew Delbanco, *College: What It Was, Is, and Should Be* (Princeton: Princeton University Press, 2012); Anthony Kronman, *Education's End: Why Our Colleges and Universities Have Given Up on the Meaning of Life* (New Haven: Yale University Press, 2008).

theoretical wisdom—as the goal of the highest and best life—is now not even a rational hope. Furthermore, practical wisdom is replaced by the modern methods of science and their academic disciplines: economics, statistics, and cognitive science. Kronman maintains that there can be no adequate understanding of the modern university and its difficulty with educating for wisdom without a clearer understanding of the twists and turns of intellectual history that have led to the present.

In "Is Wisdom Still a Value in the Academy?," Delbanco surveys the breakdown in consensus about what wisdom means. While noting the uses and abuses of equating wisdom with character, he contends that the cultivation of moral virtue is at the very heart of a university education. While Delbanco believes that the modern university often makes character formation an extracurricular activity (stationing ethical reflection in centers and institutes rather than in the classroom), he keenly illustrates efforts to educate for wisdom in several surprising places, including science labs and athletic fields. Finally, Delbanco describes the presence of a third force in the classroom. Besides teacher and student, there is what he calls "grace"—which leads, in powerful and mysterious ways, to unexpected discovery and transformation.

My essay, "The University in Crisis and the Ways of Wisdom," attempts to fashion a bridge between secular and theological proposals for wisdom education. I suggest that any attempt to teach and learn presupposes a view of human nature—about what it is to be human, how virtue might be formed, and what it is to strive for flourishing. I then explain how a Christian account of wisdom will have three aspects: practical, theoretical, and spiritual (the last understood as Divine gift.) I also imagine what it would be for the university, especially a Christian university, to foster all three kinds of wisdom.

Celia Deane-Drummond's "The Amnesia of Modern Universities: An Argument for Theological Wisdom in the Academe" suggests that the contemporary academy is shackled to Enlightenment ideals that force it into a broadly utilitarian understanding of higher education, undermining the pursuit of wisdom, especially theological wisdom. Drawing on the vision of John Henry Newman and others, Deane-Drummond contends that the wisdom of the cross can offer a corrective to a number of corrosive trends in higher education. Further, she argues for a richer sense of practical wisdom that might heighten an institution's sense of the connections among the academic disciplines, their shared effort to promote the common good, and their ultimate relation to the Divine.

John Haldane's essay "Evolution, Education, and Wisdom" explains how scientific reductionism, combined with certain ideas in evolutionary theory, poses a serious challenge to educating for wisdom in the humanities. The enormous prestige that science presently enjoys, Haldane writes, has led many to believe that science is now the ultimate mode of inquiry through which we know about the natural world, human beings, the cosmos—even the very nature of reality. Stephen Hawking, as an example, asserts that philosophy and natural theology are dead. Such hubris is best countered, according to Haldane, by education that pursues both inquiry into science *and* human beings, while appreciating, rather than collapsing, the essential difference between the two. Likewise, those who teach and learn must be reminded of the difference between knowledge and understanding; the former seeks to know the particular and the temporary, while the latter, pursing the general and the permanent, is necessary for the good human life.

The volume's final essay is Walter Brueggemann's "Slow Wisdom as a Sub-Version of Reality." Brueggemann distinguishes between two competing kinds of wisdom, each grounded in rival conceptions of who we are as human beings and what is most worthwhile to pursue. *Fast wisdom*, on one hand, assumes that humans are free to master the world around them; it presumes control. Fast wisdom is evidenced by quick forms of knowing, communicating, consuming, and possessing. *Slow wisdom*, on the other hand, which Scripture commends as rooted in "the fear of the Lord," seeks fidelity. Slow wisdom resists hurriedness; it runs counter to the culture of sound bites. It encourages deeper understanding, that comes only through patient forms of attention and relatedness. The central aim of the contemporary university,

Brueggemann writes, is to educate students in slow wisdom, to form them in the virtues of justice, righteousness, and love, especially in a time when the need for such wisdom is so pressing.

To be sure, the authors of this volume propose no quick and easy strategies to advance the cause of educating for wisdom. Yet they may do something considerably more worthwhile by helping those who care about the university to imagine what the consecration of learning might involve in the twenty-first century and beyond.

This volume grew in large measure from the 2011 Baylor Symposium on Faith and Culture, held in October of that year. I am deeply grateful to my colleagues in the Institute for Faith and Learning, whose efforts helped to make that occasion such a success, especially Jason Whitt, Ronny Fritz, and Vickie Schulz. I am likewise thankful to Joshua Hays, Rebecca Poe Hays, Heather Hughes, Joshua Jeffrey, Grant Shellhouse, and Wylie Wyman Shellhouse for their assistance during various stages of editing this book. Finally, I thank Howard K. Batson, Michael Beaty, Ron Cook, Elizabeth Davis, David Garland, Douglas Henry, David Lyle Jeffrey, L. Gregory Jones, Thomas Hibbs, James Davison Hunter, Scott Moore, W. Winfred Moore, Matt Snowden, David Solomon, Michael Stegemoller, Todd Still, Theodore Vitali, C.P., Candace Vogler, and Paul Wadell for their encouragement and friendship to me—and for their own devotion to educating for wisdom.

December 2, 2018
Waco, Texas

Wisdom in the Age of the Research Ideal
Anthony Kronman

I. Knowledge Without End

Can we educate for wisdom in the modern university? The answer seems obvious. Wisdom is perennial. So long as there are universities, there will be room in them for wisdom. This was true in Paris in the thirteenth century; it is true today at places like Baylor. But if the answer were as simple as this, I doubt this collection of essays would have been written. Indeed, there is a growing concern that there may not be, after all, much of a place for wisdom in our universities today. Why should that be?

Today a university is, above all, an institution devoted to research. Most universities of course do many other things. But the central and defining task of the modern university is to provide an organized setting for the advancement of knowledge. This is its *raison d'être*, one that extends to every discipline, including the humanities. It governs the selection of faculty, arrangement of departments, organization of curriculum, and much else besides. Everything that is most distinctive about the modern university is determined by its commitment to the research ideal.

Stated in the simplest terms, this ideal joins two beliefs. The first is that the subject matter of every discipline is always capable of being better understood than it is at present. There is no end to how far our knowledge of the subject can go. The second is that no scholar, or even generation of scholars, can ever glimpse more than a fragment of this knowledge. It accumulates over time through the successive efforts of countless researchers, each of whom adds a small bit to the collective achievements of those in his or her field, superseding the work of those who went before and expecting to be superseded in turn.

I can now reformulate my question more precisely. Why should the research ideal, as I have defined it, make anyone doubt that the teaching of wisdom has a place in our universities today? To answer this question, one needs a working definition of wisdom. I take mine from Aristotle, whose discussion of the subject has had a lasting influence on Western thought.

II. Aristotle's Account of Wisdom

Aristotle distinguishes two sorts of wisdom. One he calls theoretical and the other practical. The first has to do with those things that cannot, in his words, "be other than they are."[1] The truths of mathematics are things of this sort. But they are neither the most real nor important ones. The order of the world from the circling stars above us to the mud beneath our feet is a thing of this kind as well. It too is something that cannot be other than it is. It is necessary, and hence eternal, since what exists by necessity must remain forever unchanged. The study of this order is what Aristotle calls physics, and in its highest reaches, metaphysics. The philosopher seeks to grasp it in thought, and when he succeeds in doing so becomes, for a time, the god of the world on which his mind is eagerly trained. Nothing can possibly be more gratifying than the attainment of such wisdom. It is the highest goal toward which any human being can aim.

Practical wisdom has a different sphere of application. It is what we need to deliberate well and to make sound choices in the field of action, amidst a tumult of contingencies, where things can always be other than they are. It is a kind of discernment which enables the man or woman who possesses it to see what courage, generosity, justice, and the like require in any particular case.

---

1   Aristotle, *Posterior Analytics* 71b14–16, trans. Jonathan Barnes, Clarendon Aristotle Series, 2nd ed. (Oxford: Oxford University Press, 1994).

I want to emphasize two other features of Aristotle's account of the nature of wisdom. One concerns the perfectability of theoretical wisdom. The other has to do with the fact that practical wisdom cannot be taught. Both are explained by the distinction between form and matter—a metaphysical distinction that Aristotle takes for granted in each of his many inquiries.[2]

Every thing is a composite of form and matter. This is easy to see in the case of artifacts, whose form and matter are at first separate, then brought together by an artificer—a cobbler, for example, or a poet. But natural things are composites too. They have form and matter as well. The form of a plant or animal makes it the sort of thing it is—a starfish rather than an oyster or clam— and its matter makes it an individual member of its kind, this starfish rather than that one. Only one aspect of this composite is intelligible, however. All that we can ever know about a thing— any thing, natural or artificial—is its form. This is true whether we are talking about leather, nails and glue, or the shoe the cobbler has made; about organisms, organs, or the material of which organs are composed. At every level of inquiry, we encounter the same basic distinction between form and matter, and all that we can ever understand, at any level, is the form of the thing we are studying. Its matter, and therefore its individuality, is shapeless and therefore literally incomprehensible. No assumption lies more deeply at core of Aristotle's thought.

Aristotle's world has an inherent order or form. It is a *cosmos* in which every thing has its proper place. It is therefore inherently— and one might add, eternally—intelligible. But it is not completely intelligible, since the world contains matter as well as form. The materiality of the world renders it only partly penetrable by mind, whether ours or anyone else's. Still, everything that is intelligible in the world can be grasped by the human mind, without remainder. If we study the world with sufficient care and patience, we can understand the forms of things, and because there is nothing more to be understood about them, it is possible to acquire a knowledge of

2   See, for example, Aristotle, *Physics* II.3.

the world that is as perfect as any knowledge can be, though as mortal beings with needs, we cannot hold onto this knowledge forever. But in those contemplative moments when we grasp it, there is no higher place left for us to strive to reach. We have arrived at the summit of being. The metaphysics of form and matter ensures this.

The same metaphysics also ensures that practical wisdom cannot be taught. That is because it concerns particulars, of which, in Aristotle's view, there is perception but no knowledge. A practically wise man or woman simply sees what is right in a given situation.[3]

Only those who are virtuous have such perception. Their virtues are traits of character. A proper upbringing produces these traits, which alone make possible the moral discernment that distinguishes those with practical wisdom from the merely clever. But there is no science of practical wisdom. There is no organized body of knowledge that can instruct us how to apply the principles of virtue in any particular setting. Though it is possible to acquire practical wisdom through a process of training that welds pleasure to proper behavior, it is impossible to achieve the same goal by means of didactic instruction. The equation of intelligibility with form guarantees that particularity in general, and therefore, *a fortiori*, the sort of particularity that is relevant to our ethical and political deliberations, is something of which no one can ever have a teachable knowledge.[4]

To understand what the modern research ideal means for the pursuit of both theoretical and practical wisdom, it is essential to grasp its relation to the metaphysics of form and matter. Aristotle's account of both sorts of wisdom is based on this metaphysics. By contrast, the whole of modern science, and the research ideal which is at once its instrument and expression, rests on the dissolution of the distinction between form and matter. This represents a profound revolution in thought. But in the first instance, it is not the result of changing scientific ideas. That comes later. To begin with, it is the result of a shift in theological beliefs.

3 Aristotle, *Nicomachean Ethics* 1109b18–23.
4 Aristotle, *Nicomachean Ethics* 1104a1–9.

III. The Abrahamic Revolution

The doctrine of creation—the most basic teaching of all the Abrahamic religions—compels those who embrace it to regard the world as infinitely intelligible. A creator, unlike a craftsman, is not hostage to the imperfections of the material on which He works. There is no such material. He brings the world into being from nothing. Hence, there is nothing to impede or limit the operation of His divine mind. The world must therefore be "minded" all the way down—to the very hairs on our heads, as the Gospel says.[5] And because everything in the world is "informed" by the divine intelligence that calls it into being, the metaphysical distinction between form and matter can no longer be sustained, except as a useful fiction. It follows that the individuality of things, and not merely their general shape, must now in principle be accessible to the inquiring mind.

The shift from Aristotle's god of inherent form to the creator God of Genesis thus opens the way to the belief that there is no limit to the intelligibility of the world, and lays the ground, in every branch of human inquiry, for the supreme authority of what Leibniz calls "the principle of sufficient reason."[6] If the world is intelligible down to its smallest details, then there must be a reason why each thing is as it is. In any particular case, we may not yet know the reason, and our limitations guarantee that we shall never know all the reasons why everything is as it is. But the way is now open to an endless process of further exploration that seeks to unpack, bit by bit, the order of a world whose intelligibility is boundless, though no finite being, such as we, can ever exhaust it. This is the metaphysical meaning of the research ideal.

By dissolving the distinction between form and matter, the theological shift from paganism to Abrahamism prepares the way for

5   Matt. 10:30.
6   Leibniz, Gottfried Wilhelm. *Monadology 32, Philosophical Essays*, trans. and eds. Roger Ariew and Dan Garber (Indianapolis: Hackett, 1989), 217.

this ideal. But it simultaneously undermines the foundations of both theoretical and practical wisdom, as Aristotle conceived them, for in the absence of the distinction between form and matter, his views no longer make sense.

On the one hand, it now becomes absurd to think that with sufficient time and effort one can attain the perfect understanding of things that Aristotle still thought possible. If the world is infinitely intelligible, no one can ever get his or her mind around it all. Aristotle's ideal of theoretical wisdom falls to the ground. It is no longer even sane to seek the kind of contemplative wisdom he held up as the noblest state a human being can achieve, or to maintain that such wisdom can be taught by philosophers who already possess it.

At the same time, the belief that practical wisdom is a kind of perception, which cannot be taught because it concerns particulars, collapses as well. At any given moment, our knowledge of the particulars that affect our moral and political choices is necessarily limited. But it is a real knowledge that grows with time, and may rightly aspire to be as rigorous as any branch of human understanding. There is a genuine science of ethics, which we are slowly constructing. As a result, we no longer need to rely on virtue, and therefore on habit and character, as a foundation for correct judgment in the field of action. Practical wisdom in Aristotle's sense ceases to be the key to sound deliberation, and is replaced by scientific methods instead—by economics, for example, and statistics, and more recently by cognitive science. Our universities have an intellectual responsibility to support these disciplines. Perhaps they even have a moral duty to do so. But it is increasingly implausible to think that the promotion of more scientific decision-making has anything to do with the cultivation of practical wisdom as Aristotle understood it.

IV. Our Situation

To summarize: Aristotle's account of theoretical and practical wisdom rests on the presumed meaningfulness of a distinction between form and matter that the creationist theology of the Abrahamic religions destroys. The destruction of this distinction leads to the idea of a world that is infinitely intelligible and, with that, to the modern research ideal, which simultaneously undermines the possibility of contemplative fulfillment in the realm of theory, and the need to rely on character and habit in the field of practical action. Of course, one may attempt to rescue the spiritual value of the research ideal, which renders both sorts of wisdom moot, by insisting that it is our way of thanking God for the gift of an endlessly intelligible world—by treating research as a vocation in the old-fashioned sense of the word, so that even if the classical foundations of theoretical and practical wisdom have now been irretrievably destroyed, it is possible to believe that something of still greater value survives. But the problem with this argument is that the very theology that gave rise to the modern research ideal in the first place cannot be sustained in the teeth of the ideal's own demands and must eventually be discarded as another of those childish superstitions which the principle of sufficient reason will not allow thinking adults to retain—as Darwin courageously argued.

Our situation, then, is this. We live and work in universities dominated by the research ideal. Whatever else our universities do, they do for the sake of this. But the research ideal renders unintelligible the meaning of both theoretical and practical wisdom, as Aristotle understood them. It also swallows the revelation that inspired its own birth, and reduces the idea of a God beyond the world, whose mind we can never know, to the status of a myth, utterly incompatible with the relentless rationalism of the research ideal itself. Those who affirm that wisdom still has a place in our universities, and can in some sense be taught, therefore have an obligation to explain how the wisdom they have in mind differs from the two sorts that Aristotle describes, and from the love of God which, though still alive in many hearts, can never be regarded as anything but a private belief at war with the remorseless demands of science, when viewed from the vantage point of the research ideal and of the universities founded upon it.

This is a very tall order. One may be more or less confident about anyone's chances of filling it. But one thing, at least, is clear. We have come to our present situation by a long and twisting path, one that leads from Aristotle to Leibniz and beyond, and no one can possibly form a responsible view of it, let alone be in a position to advance or criticize views about the prospects for teaching wisdom in the universities of the twenty-first century, without some understanding of the battle of ideas that has brought us to the world we inhabit. And that, I think, is a good and sufficient reason to affirm the continuing importance of the kind of undergraduate education, increasingly unfashionable on many of our campuses, that puts the study of the West and its greatest works at the center of a sustained and wholly unembarrassed attention. For while the West may not be a better place than any other—I hardly know what such a claim could even mean—it is where the questions I have been discussing first assumed the shape they now display in every corner of the world. This will not save anyone, but it may, perhaps, help some to better understand the universities in which it is the fate of all of us to study and learn.

Is Wisdom Still a Value in the Academy?
Andrew Delbanco

When I was mulling over the key word of this volume—wisdom—it struck me that it provides both opportunities and problems, and that these might, perhaps, turn out to be the same thing. I doubt there is much controversy over the assertion that throughout the modern history of the university there has been a radical breakdown of consensus about what such a word means. The response to that breakdown, which mirrors a process in our larger society, has been to move discussion out of the public square and leave it as a matter of private conscience. Such a move tends to vitiate or at least weaken the possibility of a true discursive community; or at the very least it shrinks the range of values that an academic community can build upon. If there is an "elephant in the room" that we are not prepared to talk about with each other, then we limit our conversation to other topics. Academic freedom is a value, for instance, that academics are pretty willing to agree about, but I am afraid that is about where it begins and ends—at least in the institutions with which I am familiar.

But perhaps there are some good things about this breakdown of consensus over the meaning of such a word as wisdom. Another word comes to mind which, while not exactly cognate, is nonetheless related —namely, the word "character." Character sounds like an obviously good thing, something we should all be interested in building and nurturing. In fact, however, it is a word with a complicated history, and it can mean a lot of different things depending on how (and by whom) it is used. Not long ago I ran across a statement by the Nobel Laureate Arthur Lewis, which he made at his installation as Chancellor of the University of Guyana. In his address he lauded character as the determination "to practice the same thing over and over again while others are enjoying themselves ... to push oneself from the easy part to the hard part; to listen to criticism and use it to reject one's own work and try again."[1] Now these are indeed good qualities; I think one could say that the definition of character Lewis gives here is more or less synonymous with another good quality, stamina. This is one legitimate understanding of what "building character" would mean, and who could dispute its value?

But not so long ago in the history of our country's educational discourse, the word "character" meant something quite different. It was a thinly disguised term of discrimination intended to distinguish the model Protestant gentleman from the putatively grasping *parvenu*—in particular the importunate Jew who was seen as knocking on the college door, scheming to get into institutions where he did not, according to the reigning authorities, belong. So, for instance, early in the twentieth century, Harvard University president Abbott Lawrence Lowell proposed a "personal estimate of character" on the part of the admissions authorities, explicitly in order to control what he called "the dangerous increase in the proportion of Jews" at Harvard.[2] It was during this same period that the top floor of one of the Harvard dormitories became unaffectionately known as "Kike's Peak" because it was where many Jewish students lived. Such open bigotry may seem startling today, sanctioned as it was, rather than condemned, by the university authorities; but it is worthwhile to be startled by this kind of thing every now and again—to be reminded of the sorts of things that leading figures in our society were once willing to say not only in private but in public.

Even in the absence of such unembarrassed bigotry, however, judgments of character (which I am using as a word that carries an

---

1   Arthur Lewis, quoted by William G. Bowen in his commencement address at Indiana University, May 6, 2011.

2   Jerome Karabel, *The Chosen: The Hidden History of Admission and Exclusion at Harvard, Yale, and Princeton* (Boston: Houghton Mifflin, 2005), 51.

implication of wisdom) tend, problematically, to boil down to how comfortable the judge feels in the presence of the judged. Most people regard others as being wise or of good character to the degree that they seem to resemble themselves. In response to President Lowell's suggestion, Judge Learned Hand, a distinguished Harvard alumnus, wrote a letter in which he suggested to the president that "If anyone could devise an honest test for character, perhaps it would serve well. I doubt its feasibility except to detect formal and obvious delinquencies. Short of it, it seems to me that students can only be chosen by tests of scholarship, unsatisfactory as those no doubt are."[3] In other words universities should stop trying to measure their prospective students' virtue or probity or wisdom because such a test is by nature impossibly subjective; instead, those who demonstrate intellectual power should be admitted regardless of their presumptive wisdom or "character"—tied, in those days, at least in the minds of the gatekeepers, to their ethnicity or origin or "breeding."

Despite this history of misuse and abuse, however, I still believe there is something worth conserving in the claim, as Cardinal Newman put it in his great lectures on *The Idea of a University*, that education "implies an action upon our mental nature and the formation of a character."[4] Every university, more than merely brain-training for this or that functional task, *should* be concerned with such matters as character and wisdom. Although we may no longer agree on the attributes of virtue or wisdom as, say, codified in biblical commandments or in Enlightenment precepts, students still come to college not yet fully formed as social beings and can still be deterred from sheer self-interest toward a life of enlarged sympathy for other people and a sense of civic responsibility. Surely those qualities have something to do with what we mean by wisdom, and surely we should not be afraid of doing what we can to encourage them.

3   Quoted in James O. Freedman, *Liberal Education and the Public Interest* (Iowa City: University of Iowa Press, 2003), 107.
4   John Henry Newman, *The Idea of a University*, ed. Frank M. Turner (New Haven, CT: Yale University Press, 1996), 85.

This idea that the aim of education includes fostering ethical as well as analytical intelligence is of course not exclusively a Christian idea. It long predates the churches from which our earliest American colleges arose and is older than Christianity itself. In the Beth Midrash of Ancient Judaism, typically located physically as well as spiritually near the synagogue, students prayed for insight and clarity of mind before embarking on the day's Torah study. To join Plato's academy in Athens of the fourth century BCE was to acknowledge "a change of heart and the adoption of a new way of life via a process akin to our understanding of religious conversion."5 In first-century Rome, in Seneca's famous letter on liberal education, we find a measured yet passionate account of the power of such an education to clear the mind of "cant" by inviting it to rise above the palaver of everyday life:

> We have no leisure to hear lectures on the question of whether Odysseus was sea tossed between Italy and Sicily or outside our known world. We ourselves encounter storms of the spirit which toss us daily, and our depravity drives us into all the ills which troubled Odysseus. Show me, rather, by his example, how I am to love my country, my wife, my father, and how, even after suffering shipwreck, I'm to sail towards these ends, honorable as they are. Why try to discover whether Penelope was a pattern of purity or whether she had the laugh on her contemporaries, or whether she suspected that the man in her presence was her husband before she knew it was he? Teach me rather what purity is, and how great a good we have in it, and whether it is situated in the body or in the soul.6

5   Francis Oakley, *Community of Learning: The American College and the Liberal Arts Tradition* (New York: Oxford University Press, 1992), 50–51.

6   Seneca, *Moral Epistles*, no. 88 ("On Liberal and Vocational Studies"), 3 vols., trans. Richard M. Gummere (Loeb Classical Library) (Cambridge: Harvard University Press, 1917–1925), 2:353–355.

Alas, these sorts of questions have been dropping out of discussion and debate about the aims of university education, or at least they have been marginalized. We could discuss at length when exactly this marginalization began, but we can safely say that by the middle of the twentieth century it was well under way. In a prescient book called *The Academic Revolution* (1968), Christopher Jencks and David Riesman claimed "that moral and political questions that cannot be resolved by research, and do not yield to cooperative investigation, are almost by definition outside the academic orbit."[7] They were saying fifty years ago almost exactly what Anthony Kronman has said more recently in his fine book *Education's End*.[8]

Now our goal is to assess where we are in relation to this state of affairs, which varies no doubt from campus to campus; it will feel different at what are conventionally called faith-based institutions from how it feels at avowedly secular institutions such as Yale, NYU, or Columbia. But I think it is safe to say there is a general sense that what Jencks and Riesman were talking about has only become more pronounced. One of the symptoms of this development is that many of our academic institutions have created such subdivisions within themselves as, for instance, The Center for Human Values at Princeton, or The Institute for Ethics at Duke. These are laudable initiatives but they raise for me a troubling question: What does it mean if thinking about ethics has become an extracurricular activity? It seems that there is now a specified place to go if you have ethical questions on your mind, because such questions are not legitimately within the province of the classroom.

A recent statement more openly in a mode of lamentation comes from the former Dean of Harvard College, Harry Lewis, who points out quite rightly that many academic institutions

7 Christopher Jencks and David Riesman, *The Academic Revolution* (Piscataway, NJ: Transaction, 2001), 243.

8 Anthony T. Kronman, *Education's End: Why Our Colleges and Universities Have Given Up on the Meaning of Life* (New Haven, CT: Yale University Press, 2008).

"affect horror that students attend college in the hope of becoming financially successful, but they offer students neither a coherent view of the point of a college education or any guidance on how they might discover for themselves some larger purpose in life."[9] I would like to take a slightly more optimistic view by suggesting how some concern with ethical questions and with the problem of wisdom (How do we know it when we see it? How do we nurture it?) might still be part of the university culture.

As Kronman points out, the most conspicuous feature of modern academic culture is the rise of science. This is clearly reflected in institutional budget priorities and in the majors that students are choosing. As Kronman suggested, this trend has profound epistemological implications about what academic institutions are all about. These are institutions increasingly committed to what I would call (in perhaps too simplistic terms) a progressive theory of knowledge.

The early prevalence of this theory is evident in statements made by some of the presidents of the first full-fledged American research universities. The inaugural president of Johns Hopkins, for instance, Daniel Coit Gilman, defined not just the research mission but the teaching purpose of the new university as showing students "how to extend, even by minute accretions, the realm of knowledge."[10] Here we have a perfect example of the phenomenon Kronman describes: the explicit goal of the university is to enlarge and advance our understanding of the natural and (if we include the so-called social sciences) social world. Charles W. Eliot, the first president of Harvard whose training was in the physical sciences rather than in divinity, put it this way: "Among the most important functions of universities is to store up the accumulated knowledge of the [human] race, so that each generation of youth shall start

9   Harry Lewis, *Excellence without a Soul: How a Great University Forgot Education* (New York: Public Affairs, 2006), 17.

10   Richard Hofstadter and Wilson Smith, eds., *American Higher Education: A Documentary History*, 2 vols. (Chicago: University of Chicago Press, 1961), 2:646.

with all the advantages which their predecessors have won."[11] I call this the "relay race theory of knowledge," in which no runner ever has to travel over trodden ground.

There has been some expression of anxiety—particularly among practitioners of the humanities—about how university culture has been taken over by this principle, and I share that anxiety. Nonetheless, we ought to acknowledge that it is in fact a very powerful idea, and there are good reasons why it has been so successful. It explains, for instance, why a bright high school graduate coming into Baylor or Columbia probably has mastered at least the elementary principles of calculus, whereas in the seventeenth century, when our first institutions for higher education were founded, there were only two people in the world who had any grasp of calculus—Leibniz and Newton. That does not mean the bright sixteen-year-old today necessarily has the intellectual power of a Leibniz or Newton, but it does mean that certain kinds of knowledge can be transmitted and handed down to the next generation without having to be rediscovered or reinvented. This is a powerful truth that explains much about the power of Western culture over the last several centuries. It explains, for instance, why a third- or fourth-year medical student today will know more about the genetic basis of disease or the management of organ transplantation than the most proficient physicians or skillful surgeons knew thirty or forty years ago.

But moral knowledge, which we are here calling wisdom, does not seem to conform to this structure—at least not neatly or comfortably. We may convince ourselves that wisdom has something to do with accumulating experience, but if we are to think about transmitting or teaching wisdom in an academic context, we cannot think about it in the same way that we think about calculus or medical science. Albert Camus's 1947 novel *The Plague*, or Daniel Defoe's *Journal of the Plague Year* written in 1722, does not tell us any more about the social consequences of pestilence than Thucydides' discussion of the plague at Athens in the fifth century BCE.

11 Ibid., 2:711.

In the context of what we call the "humanities," the idea of progressive knowledge simply does not make much sense.

Given that the study of such books seems to be on the decline in most institutions—though they have not disappeared, and there are some pretty tenacious people trying to keep them going—what other repositories of wisdom might remain in the university? First of all, we must not shortchange the scientists. Many scientists I know take offense when their work is confused with the production of new technologies. Good scientists work not out of a sense of instrumental purpose but out of a sense of love: love of the incredible complexity of the natural world. They work in a mood of astonishment at nature itself, a mood that, in many cases, runs close to a sense of spiritual reverence. They tend to have humility, borne of their understanding of both the limits of what they do know and the vastness of what they do not know. (My colleague Stuart Firestein, chair of Columbia's biology department, has written a lively book on this theme entitled *Ignorance: How it Drives Science*.)[12] Ideally at least, the scientific world is a genuine open society, where people commit themselves to a collective enterprise by sharing knowledge with one another and testing one another's propositions—sometimes out of envy, I suppose, sometimes hoping that the other guy's experiment will fail or prove to be fraudulent, but more often, one hopes, with excitement and delight that new insights have been attained into subjects that had previously resisted insight. So we ought to grant our colleagues in the sciences that there is a great deal of wisdom in what they do and how they do it.

There is also a kind of wisdom inherent in the processes or what are sometimes called the "dynamics" of the classroom, even if the subject matter is not in itself directly connected to the topics of character or moral knowledge. In a class led by a skilled teacher, students learn to qualify their initial responses to hard questions; they learn the difference between informed insights and mere opinionating; they receive the pleasant chastisement of discovering that

12 Stuart Firestein, *Ignorance: How It Drives Science* (New York: Oxford University Press, 2012).

others see the world differently from them, and that their own experience is not replicable by or even reconcilable with that of others. At its best, a class can be an exercise in deliberative democracy, in which the teacher is not an orator or lawgiver but a kind of *provocateur* who gets the discussion going and shows the students what a civil discussion actually looks and feels like. One of the effects of such a class is to encourage humility—a quality that surely is one of the constituent elements of wisdom.

There is, too, a kind of wisdom to be gained from college athletics, at least when it is conducted in the right spirit. No one can be unaware of the outrageous abuses that have lately come to light in the world of college athletics. Yet some of the wisest students I have known are student athletes who already know a lot about the contingency of life, about the inevitability of failure, about the virtue of humility in victory, and about their obligations to their fellow human beings. When college athletic programs work, they make a big contribution to the work of ethical education.

In the end, I am partial, of course, to the study of the humanities as the centerpiece of the enterprise we are discussing. One of the great values of the study of history, if done properly, is that it can be an antidote to pride. When we study the past we are confronted by questions that defy simplistic answers. My own current research, for instance, is in the period just before the Civil War in the United States, when people of good conscience in all regions of the country were trying to figure out their ethical responsibilities with regard to the problem of slavery. The ones I am particularly interested in wondered whether there might be some middle way between the defense of slavery and the demand that slavery be eradicated immediately—gradual, compensated emancipation, or colonization (which to us looks much like ethnic cleansing, but which many Americans supported at the time, including African-Americans, as a way toward what we would call today the right of "self-determination")? They were looking for such a way out of the impasse over slavery because they feared civil war, and they feared that the outcome of such a war might actually be to strengthen rather than destroy slavery. By trying to get inside the minds of such figures, one of whom was Abraham Lincoln—who began his presidency as an anti-slavery man but not as an abolitionist, and who pledged in his inaugural address that he would support the fugitive slave law and ensure that that law was enforced—I think we may gain some wisdom about our own limitations and some humility as we ask ourselves what future generations will say about us. What are our moral failings? How will they look in hindsight? What obvious truths that seem conspicuous to our successors have we failed to grasp?

I have focused in these brief remarks on certain discontinuities in intellectual history and in the history of the institutions in which we work, but I want to conclude by talking very briefly about some continuities. I like to remind my students that there is a line that runs from the preacher to the teacher, and that the very term "professor" derives, after all, from the notion of a faith community. Whether we like it or not, all of us in academia have inherited that tradition and are still, in some ways, beholden to it.

But in the mostly post-theistic academic world that many of us inhabit, those kinds of assumptions often seem remote, even bizarre, to professors and students alike. One way I try to address this question is as follows. Every real teacher knows that apart from teacher and student there is a third force in the room. It is a mysterious force, which sometimes acts on the mind of the student in a way that awakens him or her to a new insight or maybe even to a whole new way of thinking about life. At other times nothing of the sort happens. You can give the best lecture you have ever given and ask the most provocative questions you have ever asked, and some of the students in the room will just stare at you and wonder what time it is and when they can escape. But perhaps somebody in the back row who may not have said anything for the whole semester will come up to you afterwards or to your office hour and ask to go further into the subject at hand. And sometimes that student, by surprise, and without any pre-formulated strategy or plan—even without conscious effort—has had a transformative experience. In the tradition from which many faith-based college and universities have emerged, and to which many of their students still belong, the theological word for this inaudible and invisible force is grace. In my institution, by contrast, not many students come from a background where this term "grace" is familiar. So in order to explain the idea I use an analogy that—while doubtless defective—captures, at least for me, the heart of the matter.

Imagine that two college roommates go out one evening to see a production of King Lear—a play about an old man cruelly duped by his own children, who is losing his grip on power, dignity, and even his own senses, and who ends up wandering alone under the open sky without shelter, or mercy, or hope. These two roommates go and see a local production of the play, and when it ends they come out of the theater and one of them says to the other, "You know, that was really kind of a waste of time. I don't know what the big deal was, that old guy really had it coming to him. He's an unbearable whiner. I didn't want to listen to him any longer. Let's go get a beer." Meanwhile, the other young man has had a devastating experience. He doesn't know why, he doesn't know how, but he finds himself thinking about his own father, about the obligation of children to parents, and for that matter of parents to children, about the savage sadness that comes upon many people in their broken old age; in fact, he finds himself thinking about every aspect of his life in a new way. Does he want to have children of his own? If so, how will he bring them up? Maybe he thinks about becoming a physician, or maybe he just wants to call home to see how his father, with whom he's had a difficult relationship, is doing; or, more likely, he doesn't know what to do but he feels the sudden conviction that his plans and priorities need to be revisited and revised. One thing he knows for sure is that he doesn't want to end up like Lear wandering alone on the heath. In short, the world has been transformed for him while it remains utterly unchanged for his friend. And yet these two young men have heard the same voices and words, seen the same bodies and props moving about on the stage, or to put it in mechanistic terms, they have experienced the same aural and visual stimuli.

I think it is impossible to say why something so important has happened to one of these young men and not to the other. Their

SAT scores may be identical; in fact, the one whom the play leaves unmoved may have higher scores, better grades, and better prospects to make the Dean's List. The difference between them is immeasurable by any testing instrument and has nothing to do with which one has studied harder for tomorrow's exam on Elizabethan drama. Many of us who work in education today have no language to account for this mystery—the mystery of why one of them takes a step toward wisdom and the other does not. We have no language for it, but that doesn't mean the mystery doesn't exist. My point is that if something like that can happen—and it can happen in a lecture, it can happen in a discussion, it can happen in a theatrical performance—then maybe it is a kind of wisdom to know that we control very little of the effects of what we do, including our efforts to define and grasp wisdom for ourselves or to impart it to others.

The University in Crisis
and the Ways of Wisdom
Darin H. Davis

Even casual observers of American higher education recognize that the contemporary academy is in the midst of great challenge and transformation.[1] The cost of a college degree continues to increase by leaps and bounds as many students and their parents assume enormous student loan debt.[2] Not long ago a college degree nearly guaranteed financial success and career stability. Those days seem over. Some people wonder if the days of traditional classroom teaching and learning are over as well. Sweeping technological change, especially online instruction, is now forcing colleges and universities to re-envision how course content can be offered to students.[3] These are by no means the only signs that the academy is experiencing both change and stress.

---

1   Among recent books that lament the present state of higher education are: Derek Bok's *Our Underachieving Colleges*; Harry Lewis's *Excellence Without a Soul*; William G. Bowen, Matthew M. Chingos, and Michael S. McPherson's *Crossing the Finish Line: Completing College at America's Public Universities*; and Richard Arum and Josipa Roksa's *Academically Adrift: Limited Learning on College Campuses*.

2   Glenn Harlan Reynolds, "Degrees of Value: Making College Pay Off: For Too Many Americans, College Today Isn't Worth It," *The Wall Street Journal* (February 2, 2015), http://online.wsj.com/news/articles/SB10001424052 7023038707045792983026378020002?mg=reno64-wsj&url= http%3A%2F%2Fonline.wsj.com%2Farticle%2FSB 1000142405270 2303870704579298302637802002.html .

3   See William G. Bowen, *Higher Education in the Digital Age* (Prince-

Amid these developments, it is not clear what people expect colleges and universities to do in the first place. Should they be primarily devoted to preparing their graduates to enter the workforce? Should they at the same time advance innovative research across the disciplines in ways that expand the frontiers of knowledge? Should they seek to form their students intellectually, morally, and even spiritually while preparing them for responsible citizenship and civic engagement? Should they also be the places where enthusiastic sports fans gather in grand arenas and stadiums to watch athletes pursue victory? The answer seems to be a resounding "yes" to all of these. But with so many competing expectations from so many constituencies (students, faculty, administrators, governing boards, alumni, accreditation agencies, governmental authorities, and the marketplace) it is no wonder that the academy seems to be suffering an *identity* crisis, or perhaps something akin to cognitive dissonance. Perhaps some of the current challenges in higher education could be better navigated if some of these expectations were scrutinized and prioritized. This, however, would require asking even more basic questions.

A generation ago it was generally believed that the *essential* purpose of a university education involved shaping both the moral and intellectual character of students in ways that led them to live and do well over their entire lives. I take this to be what is intended by the phrase "educating for wisdom." In the contemporary milieu of American higher education, however, such a claim will seem to some irrelevant. Still others may have little idea of what wisdom actually is, perhaps confusing it with shrewdness or ingenuity. So before any proposal about educating for wisdom can receive serious consideration, careful thinking needs to be done about what wisdom is, and how the pursuit of it might direct the aims of education. Beyond this, there is a need to reflect upon the nature of the crisis experienced by the modern academy. My own sense is

ton, NJ: Princeton University Press, 2013) and Jeffrey J. Selingo, *College Unbound: The Future of Higher Education and What It Means for Students* (New York: Amazon Publishing, 2013).

that the crisis is of a spiritual nature, that the university's very soul is in disarray.

I. Remembering Ancient Wisdom

Wisdom is a complex notion that resists simple definition. But a good first step is to recall how the ancient Greek tradition, particularly the philosophical works of Plato and Aristotle, understood wisdom, and how their conception of wisdom is embedded in a larger account of what it is to be human.

The Greek tradition understood wisdom as a virtue (*arête*), an excellence that enables one to strive for true flourishing or happiness (*eudaimonia*). Though Plato and Aristotle believed that humans are neither morally good nor bad by nature, they maintained that humans can become good by developing, though habituation, a "second nature" of virtue. Virtues become a stable part of one's character not in an instant, but over time and through experience. The virtue of honesty, for example, comes from being truthful time and again; through the process of habituation one becomes an honest person. The temperate person, through the use of reason, controls her desires consistently, not just every once in a while.

Two preliminary points might be made regarding the relationship between virtue and education. First, one acknowledges that an education aimed toward wisdom or any other virtue is not quickly or easily achieved. Happiness, as the Greeks envisioned it, is to be judged over the course of an entire human life, not in individual acts or episodes. So the formation of virtue is quite literally the work of a lifetime, not a single semester or even a four-year span in the university. At best, any attempt to educate for virtue is like an initiation, a way of setting forth an itinerary that one will follow for the rest of one's life.

Second, because happiness, on this view, is an all-encompassing notion of a life well lived, the formation of virtue is not easily accounted for in so-called "learning outcomes," at least not the sort than can be measured with precision through assessment tools. As Aristotle explained near the beginning of his *Nicomachean Ethics*, we can only expect as much precision as the subject matter allows.[4] But the lack of a measurement tool for virtue need not deter the effort to make it the fundamental goal of education. The most important components of an enduringly happy life, whether personally or socially considered, are qualitative rather than quantitative in nature, and so resist the kind of assessment that professional educational administrators often feel drawn to as a means of justification.

So what kind of virtue is wisdom, and on what basis may we justify the pursuit of it? Broadly construed, the ancient Greek tradition conceived of wisdom in two aspects, practical and theoretical. Practical wisdom involves knowing what to do—as well as how and when to do it—all in a way that is consistent with human flourishing. Navigating a difficult situation with a co-worker, finding the best way to offer advice to a friend in distress, or determining the best way to act courageously in a dangerous situation—all of these require practical wisdom. Practical wisdom is expressed in action. But practical wisdom depends first and foremost on one's ability to rightly *see* the circumstances one faces. There is no good way of knowing what, how, and when to act unless one can sensitively appreciate the context in which one will act. In this way, practical wisdom is necessary for the full expression of any of the other virtues.

But the practically wise person not only has a well-tuned moral perception; she also can deliberate well about the best way to achieve the goal she sees as good. To achieve a certain goal, one needs both a conception of what is being pursued and an understanding of how best to achieve it. Accordingly, practical wisdom is aptly described as goal-directed reason and is required for any act of virtue whatsoever. It is important to remember that, for Aristotle, practical wisdom was not just one among a long list of virtues. Instead, the practically wise person (*phronimos*) is the norm and standard of virtue.[5] The one who is truly wise has moral

---

4   See Aristotle, *Nicomachean Ethics*, I.3.
5   Aristotle, *NE*, II.7, 1106b36-1107a2, trans. Barnes.

vision, the deliberative power to choose well, and then goes on to do what is virtuous.

But seeing, deliberating, and doing the right thing in a *particular* circumstance also involves grasping a more *general* understanding of what is good. This more general conception depends on one having theoretical wisdom. The Greek insight here is that one cannot know what is best to do in a particular circumstance without knowing what is best more generally.

In the Greek tradition, theoretical wisdom is described in a number of important texts. Consider, for instance, Book VII of Plato's *Republic* and the allegory of the cave. Recall that the lone cave dweller is unshackled from chains of self-imposed ignorance and begins the long, painful ascension towards the ineffable form of the Good, the source of all that is true, good, and beautiful—Being itself. Aristotle likewise describes a longing that all humans have for this more general kind of wisdom. In his *Metaphysics*, he expresses the yearning to know things at their most general level as the expression of a natural desire—a sense of wonder that all humans have. The particulars we know through the senses "do not tell us the 'why' of anything."[6] Yet we desire to know why. So we inquire into the *cause* of the particular things, including ourselves. We seek to understand, to unify disparate elements of experience, to find meaning. This kind of inquiry is aimed ultimately at understanding the Divine, which for Aristotle was an unmoved mover, the first cause of the universe. Theoretical wisdom, therefore, was an exercise of the most divine element in us towards the most divine object. As Aristotle put it, we are to "take on immortality as much as possible."[7] This description of wisdom is something akin to a conversion. Again, wisdom is not just one among many virtues; it is preeminent.

It is important to realize that the Greek understanding of practical and theoretical wisdom is grounded in a larger conception of human nature. Human beings are complex, both physiologically

6   Aristotle, *Met.* I.1, 981b112–13, trans. Barnes.
7   Aristotle, *NE*, X.7, 1177b30-1178.2, trans. Barnes.

and psychologically. We desire things that keep us alive at a very fundamental level (things like food, drink, and sex); but we also desire power, honor, wealth, friendship, and knowledge. Our desires have to be rightly ordered, and so it is the role of reason (our powers of reflection, deliberation, and intelligence) to direct us to our proper end—living and doing well over a complete human life. The ancients clearly placed supreme confidence in the power of reason; it alone was capable of ordering human action, of shaping human desire, of reflecting upon truth, beauty, and goodness. Likewise, the ancients pointed the *telos* of human life internal to human life itself, not toward any eternal world. There may be an immortal world—the realm of the gods, the unmoved mover, the forms—but this is not where human happiness is pursued. If the Greeks were right, then there can be no more important task for education than to seek and cultivate wisdom, for wisdom is the virtue that helps orient humans toward *eudaimonia*. But is this possible today?

II. Can Wisdom Be Found in the Modern University?

At first glance, it might appear that many colleges and universities are in fact educating for wisdom—practical wisdom at least—through the myriad courses and programs in leadership studies and applied ethics that have cropped up, especially in the last two decades. Nested in the curricula of business schools, education departments, and other professional programs, these programs often promise to prepare students for ethical decision making and problem solving, civic engagement, and global leadership. These aspirations doubtlessly require practical wisdom, though these programs rarely describe themselves as forming students in wisdom *per se*.

But, despite admirable intentions, such initiatives actually undermine practical wisdom unless they are properly conceived. One way such courses can be ill-conceived is to promise students techniques, skills, and tools that they can use to achieve success in a particular domain, particularly in their role as "ethical leaders." On its face, this may seem like an entirely noble aspiration. If students are preparing to confront the challenges inherent in a complex world, a good education should provide the necessary tools to take with them along the way. But the bare mention of techniques, skills, and tools is problematic. The sort of moral reflection that is part of practical wisdom is not a handy, multi-purposed tool or a five-step technique that can be applied to solve moral quandaries. Although virtues and skills are *both* developed through consistent practice, one can be skillful in any number of pursuits (e.g., fly fishing, wood carving, tennis playing, or playing the stock market) and still be a crook, a liar, and a cheat. Stated simply, virtues are about more than performing particular activities well; they are about *being* the right sort of person. This is the central reason that formation for any kind of virtue requires special attention, and why formation in practical wisdom cannot be like the assembly of a well-equipped tool kit. Virtues, unlike tools, are not the sorts of things that can be taken up, used, and put away. Virtues are internal dispositions that shape one's entire way of living.

These "tool kit" courses in leadership and applied ethics proliferate because know-how questions dominate the psyche of the contemporary university. The engines of the modern university are churning briskly—producing mountains of research, readying students to enter the work force—but the techniques and tools being refined and the knowledge being passed down to the next generation are rarely appraised up and against more general moral commitments. These commitments can only themselves be understood through the pursuit of something akin to what the Greeks understood as theoretical wisdom. Indeed, if it has not entirely disappeared from the consciousness of contemporary higher education, theoretical wisdom is unquestionably in exile, found in rather failing health in the care of philosophy departments. But even in philosophy departments, where one might expect to find the pursuit of fundamental questions in full bloom, hyper-specialization wins the day, as the projects of moral philosophers and metaphysicians seem to be not so much at cross purposes but wholly unrelated, quite contrary to the vision of philosophy practiced by Plato, Aristotle, and others. [8] Indeed, the impoverishment of theoretical wisdom seems to go hand in glove with hyper-specialization. It is not just that scientists and scholars of the humanities do not talk much about higher-order questions; it is that scholars and teachers hardly speak to anyone outside of their own disciplinary specialization. It is hard to cultivate anything like wisdom under such conditions.

The trickle-down effect to students is lamentable. The vision of a university education that they receive is largely utilitarian, consumerist, and fragmented. Precisely when there is more need than ever for a reconciliation of practical wisdom and theoretical wisdom—to model for the wider culture that wise action requires serious reflection on essential questions of meaning—the university seems not at all able to lead in that regard.

As a practical matter, not all students need to pursue advanced degrees in philosophy to become formed in theoretical wisdom. Rather, colleges and universities need to attend to the ways that philosophical questions pervade human experience and can be found at literally every turn in a student's education. What would it mean if more courses were taught in ways that encouraged scholars and students to think outside the bounds of their own subject matter and in ways that attempted to integrate larger concerns shared among the disciplines? Or imagine if students received the message from their very first days on campus that they would be encouraged and indeed *expected* to *slow down*, ask essential questions about human life, read and discuss great texts that explore these questions among good teachers and other students—not because these endeavors would earn them a six-figure salary after graduation, but because it might orient their lives towards authentic happiness?

An education that prizes wisdom would not lead necessarily to the expansion of philosophy departments. It would, however, mean that inherently philosophical questions would be vibrantly and

8   Alasdair MacIntyre, *God, Philosophy, and Universities: A Selective History of the Catholic Philosophical Tradition* (Lanham, MA: Rowman & Littlefield, 2009), 17–18.

realistically presented throughout the activities of a university education and that there would be a set of central concerns that no one seeking an integrated life could possibly avoid. It is lamentable that precisely this kind of education, so direly needed to help meet the most essential needs of students, is nearly non-existent in most institutions of higher learning these days.

III. How Christians Understand Wisdom

The model of educating for wisdom sketched so far is broadly in line with the kind of reform urged for so persuasively by secular humanists like Anthony Kronman and Andrew Delbanco.[9] This conception of liberal education—the deep engagement with the fundamental questions of human meaning—would do much to counter the prevalent notion that a college education is primarily about preparing students to enter the workforce. As Delbanco writes, "[A]n American college is only true to itself when it opens its doors to all—rich, middling, and poor—who have the capacity to embrace the precious chance to think and reflect before life engulfs them."[10] An education animated by the search for wisdom would extend the horizon and reach of students, initiating them into a lifelong pursuit of moral and intellectual excellence, helping them to make sense of who they are and should become.

But there is a distinctive way that education pursued from the perspective of the Christian faith might seek and cultivate wisdom, and it, too, is worthy of consideration as another model of learning that might serve as a counterweight to the prevailing trends in the modern academy. Indeed, given the way that Christian learning extends from the very founding of the medieval university at Paris

---

9   See Anthony Kronman, *Education's End: Why Our Colleges and Universities Have Given Up on the Meaning of Life* (New Haven: Yale University Press, 2007), and Andrew Delbanco, *College: What it Was, Is, and Should Be* (Princeton, NJ: Princeton University Press, 2012).

10 Delbanco, *College: What it Was, Is, and Should Be*, 35.

and Salamanca; to the establishment of American universities like Harvard, Yale, and Princeton; and to the present day at schools that are diverse both in size, aspiration, and expression of faith commitment, a Christian understanding of liberal learning deserves special attention. Such an account of higher education will recognize not only practical and theoretical wisdom (as Kronman and Delbanco do); it also will seek a third kind of wisdom—theological, or spiritual wisdom.

Because of its very nature, and because of the limits of human perception and language, any description of divinely ordered wisdom is bound to be incomplete. It would be helpful, however, to see how a broadly Christian conception of human nature and virtue differs from the views of the Greeks. The differences, though drawn very broadly here, will reveal some of what is distinctive about spiritual wisdom.

First, Christians hold a doctrine of creation for which the Greeks had no equivalent. The book of Genesis recounts that humans come into existence through the intentional creative act of God, the creator of the heavens and earth. All other living creatures were created according to their kind, but God creates human beings in His own likeness and image (*imago Dei*) and blesses them in a special way.[11] But a Christian account of human nature also has a distinctive account of the end or goal of human life. The Divine is not only the source of creation; it is also what all human beings ultimately seek as their *telos*, as the perfection of their nature. In the Gospel of John, Christ proclaims that He is the way, the truth, and the life. In the book of Revelation, Christ declares, "I am the Alpha and the Omega, the Beginning and the End, the First and the Last."[12] Accordingly, for Christians, perfect happiness is not simply living and doing well in *this* life, but rather *beatitudo*, the personal union of human beings with the Divine in the eternal life to come.

The Christian account of creation and teleology has important implications for the confidence that can be placed in the powers of

11 Gen. 1:27–28.
12 John 14:6; Rev. 22:13.

human reason. For example, in the very first question of his *Summa Theologica,* Aquinas speaks to this precise point. It is necessary for human salvation, Aquinas explains, that there should be a knowledge that is revealed by God instead of by reason.[13] Philosophical science, as Aquinas terms it, powered by human intelligence, has a limit. About this, the ancients and Aquinas agree. But for the Greeks, human reason is, in the end, *all* that humans have. Though reason will be inevitably exhausted when it reaches the rarified air of the Divine, human beings in the end must accept that transcendence, construed as an escape from the clutches of the temporal world, is simply not to be. Yet Christians believe there is the hope of transcendence, not achieved by the rational capacities of the self but rather offered as divine grace through Christ's resurrection. Accordingly, when Christians recognize the limits of human reason they do not accept it with only Stoic-like resignation. Instead, Christians acknowledge that certain truths are *necessarily* beyond reason and therefore must be received as a divine gift.

Indeed, the fact of human limitation transforms a Christian understanding of virtue, and accordingly wisdom. For the Greeks, human flourishing is to be pursued through sheer human effort, through the habituation of *acquired virtue.* But for Christians, true happiness, envisioned as *beatitudo,* is beyond the grasp of frail human beings. Yet the acceptance of human finitude does not lead to a fatalism regarding the human condition. Christians see divine grace as the singular means to achieve perfect happiness. Grace bridges the chasm between human nature *as it is* and human nature *as it may become,* transformed in the light of the wisdom of God. Accordingly, divine wisdom is, in Aquinas's language, an *infused virtue,* God acting through humans moving them towards the perfection of their nature.[14]

Christians, thus, recognize three forms of wisdom: practical, theoretical, and spiritual—the latter surpassing the first two because it issues forth from God. The Christian faith is deeply

13 *Summa Theologica* I, Q.1, Art.1.
14 *Summa Theologica* II, Q. 45.

steeped, of course, in the wisdom tradition of the Old Testament, where the imagination of the good life extends to what orthodox Jews would call "the life to come." The book of Proverbs, most notably, is a sustained message about the necessity of discerning and following the wisdom of God and how those who do will find happiness.[15] Spiritual wisdom brings human beings a more distinct awareness of how God is not only manifest in all of creation, but also the particular ways that God calls each person to faithfulness. Such wisdom can never come from sheer intellectual effort alone because it surpasses what can ever be grasped through the power of cognition. This is not to say that reason plays no role in the discernment of spiritual wisdom. Rather, grace perfects reason, revealing a transcendent source of guidance that outstrips the powers of human understanding.

So what are some particular ways that spiritual wisdom might shape the teaching and learning of Christians? First, an education that seeks and affirms spiritual wisdom should reveal connections and interdependence among the academic disciplines. While the contemporary academy is often described as a "multiversity" where fragmentation abounds and the various disciplines lack a common language with which to speak to one another, Christians have a special reason to resist this trend.[16] The reason that Christian teachers and scholars might realize relationships among their subjects is not simply a matter of referring to themselves as Christian economists or Christian sociologists or anything else. Instead, the reason is ontological in nature, built into the fabric of a Christian conception of reality. If divine wisdom is the very wellspring of all teaching and learning (i.e., if God is the creative source of all goodness, truth, and beauty), then each academic discipline, as it seeks to discover that source of truth, will in some way find relation to other lines of inquiry that seek the same end. In this way, scholarly teaching and learning, no matter its point of departure, reveals an aspect of the Divine.

15 Prov. 3:13 (NKJV).
16 Wendell Berry, "The Loss of the University," in *Home Economics* (New York: North Point Press, 1987), 76–97.

For example, a colleague of mine in electrical engineering frequently teaches a course on solar energy in an especially interesting way. Besides teaching principles and applications in electrical engineering, he also encourages students to reflect about matters involving God's creation, human consumption and conservation, Christian views of stewardship, etc. These questions seek engagement with other academic disciplines, including theology, philosophy, economics, and environmental science. Accordingly, a Christian conception of learning that seeks spiritual wisdom as its goal may show not only how seemingly disparate disciplines are related; it also can reveal how disciplines actually depend on one another.

Further, on a Christian view, the pursuit and cultivation of spiritual wisdom should be marked by charity (*caritas*), the love of God and love of neighbor. To some, this may sound like rhetorical flourish or some kind of hopelessly naive aspiration, especially in the context of contemporary higher education. But for Christians, educating for spiritual wisdom through the various activities of teaching, learning, research, and scholarship should be a profound expression of love for God and neighbor. It is out of God's providential love that humans are created; likewise, it is because of God's love that He calls humans to genuine happiness, to the perfection of their nature. Accordingly, seeking and receiving spiritual wisdom is precisely what God made humans to do: to understand, however incompletely, the love of God and the way God calls His creatures to faithfulness. Likewise, those who educate for the sake of spiritual wisdom will see others (teachers, students, colleagues, co-investigators) as fellow lovers of truth, created also to seek and understand God's wisdom. Undoubtedly the ways that charity might inspire the aims of education could be countercultural. Both the subject matter of one's study and one's intellectual collaborators would be objects of love, worthy of attention and care. Teaching and learning would be more akin to prayer and worship and less like efforts to "master" a particular body of knowledge for the sake of self.[17]

17 Paul J. Griffiths, "From Curiosity to Studiousness: Catechizing the Appetite for Learning," *Teaching and Christian Practices: Reshaping*

Third, an education animated by spiritual wisdom can encourage in teachers and learners a profound sense of awe and humility. The very recognition of a creative source of truth, goodness, and beauty that stands independent of time, place, and circumstance puts human intelligence, and its limits, in proper perspective. Humans are prone to all kinds of failures of perception, misunderstanding, and plain and simple error when they seek to teach, learn, and understand. Beyond the intellectual mistakes that abound, moral and spiritual vice can cloud efforts to realize what is true and best. But the awareness of human fallibility need not lead to despair. For Christians, human imperfection instead provokes a sense of awe, understood as the remarkable mix of fear, wonder, and reverence experienced when one acknowledges something truly real, powerful, and beautiful beyond oneself.[18] It is through this recognition of the Divine that awe begets humility, as one comes to realize the proper relationship between oneself, others, and God. And from humility, there comes obedience to the divine will, so that one orders his intellect, affections, and actions towards the fulfillment of genuine happiness.

IV. The University in Spiritual Disorder?

Christian humanists like Celia Deanne-Drummond, John Haldane, Walter Brueggemann, and others share the same concerns about American higher education as secular humanists like Kronman and Delbanco do. While the general diagnosis of the problem is largely the same, their views diverge about the exact nature of the prescription. Secular humanists and Christian humanists may well agree that the best remedy is wisdom, but they may also part company once they begin to explore the various ways of understanding what wisdom is. These differences are likely to grow out of distinct

---

Faith and Learning, ed. David I. Smith and James K. A. Smith (Grand Rapids, MI: Wm. B. Eerdmans, 2011), 102–122.

18 The connection between fear and wisdom is powerfully made in Ps. 111:10: "The fear of the Lord is the beginning of wisdom." (NKJV)

conceptions of what it is to be human. No theory of education can be neutral about such matters.

For all that, there is good reason for secular humanists and Christian humanists to engage in rigorous argument about questions concerning views of human nature and the aims of education. But there is also good reason to believe that American higher education is presently in such a precarious predicament that secular humanists and Christians should acknowledge the commitments they hold in common and join forces, as it were, for the sake of recovering the university's sense of its noble calling.

But perhaps there is even more to reclaim than the academy's original sense of mission. The modern university both shapes and is shaped by the larger culture—by long-held practices and fleeting trends. This is important to consider when reflecting upon the condition of the university: it is distracted, moving in so many directions, trying to fulfill the wants and desires of so many competing constituencies, that it does not have a grounded sense of its responsibility to educate for wisdom. Indeed, the modern university seems to be exhibiting a kind of spiritual disorder, its very soul compromised. The crisis I am describing draws attention to a larger cultural malaise. If this is so, what might be the nature of this disorder?

Among the seven deadly sins in the Christian tradition is *acedia*.[19] Often taken to be laziness or sloth, *acedia* literally means to be without care, to be infused with an apathy and indifference rooted in the conviction that nothing really matters. Opposed to

19 Aquinas deals with this deadly sin in *Summa*, II-II, Q.35. I should acknowledge that the conditions for pursuing theoretical wisdom come especially difficult today, given the fast-paced, information-driven state of near constant distraction in which we live. Paul Wadell and I have touched on this in our essay "Tracking the Toxins of Acedia: Re-envisioning Moral Education," in *The Schooled Heart: Moral Formation and American Higher Education*, ed. Michael D. Beaty and Douglas V. Henry (Waco, TX: Baylor University Press, 2007), 133–156.

the virtue of magnanimity (of being "great-souled"), *acedia* is giving up the conviction that anything truly noble is worth pursuing; it is a spiritual malaise that saps one's sense of hope. The good, the true, the beautiful—whatever is excellent—are seen as simply too high to attain. So those who have succumbed to *acedia* turn away from what is best and noble and try to busy themselves in pursuing "counterfeit goods" instead. They are drawn especially to distraction by trivial things, wastes of time and energy that are not conducive to authentic happiness. Those with *acedia* seek whatever they imagine will take their minds off what they have come to perceive as the hopelessness of their task. It is a means of coping, a way of settling for much less than they were meant to be, but also the recipe for suffering a true identity crisis. *Acedia* is the general condition of much of university culture, and to destructive effect.

Admittedly, the category of *acedia* is by itself insufficient to account for the state of the contemporary university, much less to the larger culture. But if the university suffers from the kind of disorder that many think it does, its challenges are far more complicated than they might first appear. No new technique, strategy, or additional assessment measurement is likely to address the pressing challenges the modern academy faces. Determining the way forward will require wisdom.

The Amnesia of Modern Universities: An Argument for Theological Wisdom in the Academe[1]
Celia Deane-Drummond

I. Introduction

This essay draws primarily on my experience of working in the United Kingdom university sector, where for seventeen years I was based in the University of Chester, founded in 1839 by the Church of England, mainly to train teachers in order to facilitate the education of poor communities in the northwest of England. Although the university still has a Christian ethos built into its mission statement, this in itself has generated some controversy; like other higher educational establishments in the UK, it still attracts government funding. It also expanded its brief from a higher education college dedicated to educating teachers to one that offered not just education degrees but those specifically tailored for a variety of professions, including nursing, subjects allied to medicine, law, drama, and Christian ministry, as well as more traditional academic subjects such as mathematics, modern languages, history, English, biological sciences, and geography.

---

1   While this chapter draws on the following earlier work, it includes new elements and is thoroughly revised; C. Deane-Drummond, "Wisdom Remembered, Recovering a Theological Vision for Wisdom in the Academe," in *Wisdom in the University*, ed. Ronald Barnett and Nicholas Maxwell (London: Routledge, 2008), 77–88.

While the UK is not as secular as some other parts of Europe, theology and even religious studies departments struggle to be recognized as valid academic disciplines in their own right. This applies even in those higher education colleges which have a Christian foundation, exemplified by the loss of the theology degree at Cheltenham and Gloucestershire College of Higher Education, which, like Chester, became a university in its own right under the name of Gloucestershire University early on at the turn of the twenty-first century. Fortunately, the department of theology and religious studies at Chester was not under threat during my time in the department. Whereas other theology departments have shrunk or disappeared, such as those at Bangor University and the University of Wales at Lampeter, Chester University managed overall to expand its staff to student ratio and widen its doctoral provision for theology and religious studies students. But this growth is unusual, and overall the status of theology and religious studies in the academic community in the UK more generally is low, or simply ignored. This impinges on the way social scientists conduct their research, for many have been slow to appreciate the importance of religion in shaping public opinion.

I will use an example from my own experience working with internationally recognized social scientists in the late 1990s at Lancaster University who were concerned with what was motivating public opinion around genetically modified crops, a heavily contested political issue at the time. The published report on public opinion on this issue, entitled *Uncertain World*, contained virtually no reference to religion.[2] When I went through these transcripts with a social science colleague at the University of Lancaster who was far more sympathetic to religious issues, it soon became clear that implicit religious issues were actually highly significant in shaping public opinion, and this sparked a joint journal article and a

---

2   R. Grove White, P. Macnaghten, S. Meyer, and B. Wynne, *Uncertain World: Genetically Modified Organisms, Food and Public Attitudes in Britain* (Lancaster: Centre for the Study of Environmental Change, Lancaster University, 1999).

conference.[3] This short story illustrates a number of issues. In the first place, the fact that religion was initially ignored shows that recognizing religion as a topic even worth investigating was marginal to the thinking of many serious academics, at least in the UK. Second, it reflects a more general forgetfulness about the place of theology in the academe.

In those places where religious studies are accepted as a subject discipline, they tend to ape other areas of science and be treated methodologically as a detached academic discipline in order to try to give them greater credibility. Theology is even more the Cinderella subject, often appearing as a laughing stock to other academics (as illustrated in David Lodge's popular fictional novel depicting the University of Rummage—possibly the code name for England's University of Birmingham, which actually has a respectable theology department).[4] As a scientist in the 1980s, my own interest in theology attracted a certain amount of derision from scientific colleagues; although this was mostly good humored, it reflected a subtle distaste for associating religious belief with university education.[5] This is a far cry from theology's role as "queen of the sciences" in the thirteenth century. Even in Britain, arguably a largely secular society, the public remembers, if only implicitly, the long history of religious experience that is embedded in its consciousness. This surfaces in the

3   This was published in Celia Deane-Drummond, Robin Grove White and Bronislaw Szerszynski, "Genetically Modified Theology: The Religious Dimensions of Public Concerns About Agricultural Biotechnology," *Studies in Christian Ethics* 14 no. 2 (2001): 23–41; and also in book form in C. Deane-Drummond and B. Szerszynski, eds., *Re-Ordering Nature: Theology, Society and the New Genetics* (London: T&T Clark/Continuum, 2003).

4   David Lodge, *Paradise News* (London: Secker and Warburg, 1991).

5   I was given jokingly the nickname of Cedd, which of course are my initials, but Cedd (620–664) was also a well-known Celtic Christian missionary to Northumbria, a region that is more expansive than present day Northumberland, and took in Durham where I lived and worked.

recognition of the importance of religious concerns for informing the way we live, however far they may be from traditional theological formulations. I suggest that attempts to suppress this wisdom come about, at least in part, from the captivity of universities to a narrowly conceived Enlightenment agenda that has served simply to reinforce a utilitarian model for education. Ideologies including Fascism, Communism, scientific naturalism, and capitalism all had a part to play in excluding theology from the academic curriculum. There are other factors at play as well in squeezing theology out in the twentieth century—sharp and highly influential critics included Marx, Feuerbach, Nietzsche, Freud, and a host of others were also reacting against the once domineering role of the church in university life.[6] While to some extent the Enlightenment cry for liberation from ecclesial authority is perfectly understandable given the former considerable power of the church over university life, the pendulum has now swung the other way, so that one kind of captivity replaces another. In its more aggressive form the new atheism of Richard Dawkins, Daniel Dennett, and others is determined to excise theology not only from the agenda of universities, but also from public life as well.

In fact, in order to survive, theology has often been forced to capitulate to the academic agenda dictated by its secular partners. Students are now asked to make sense of Scripture, instead of Scripture making sense of them. The lack of attention to Scripture filters down to high school education. Even those students coming to explicitly Christian colleges seem to lack an adequate grounding in Scripture, at least from the report of Philip Ryken, President of Wheaton College.[7] Theology becomes "domesticated and secularized"; and, perhaps most important of all, theology is prised apart from praxis, so that skills learned in theology are now named as

---

6   As discussed in David Ford, *The Future of Christian Theology* (Oxford: Wiley/Blackwell, 2011), 95.

7   As reported at the Presidents' Panel, Friday October 28, *Educating for Wisdom in the 21ˢᵗ Century Symposium*, Baylor University, 2011.

"transferable skills."[8] Could one say with Walter Brueggemann that by cutting loose from its moorings in historical and lived reality, theology simply joins in the chorus of the most powerful, the "fast" wisdom that is joined with might and wealth?[9] Is this a betrayal of Christian hope that is committed to fidelity, a slow wisdom that waits, watches, and hopes? Those engaged in religious studies take this detachment from ancient ideals still further, so that students are encouraged to keep an entirely neutral stance toward religions, combined with a supposedly objective approach to their studies. But, ask the critics, surely such neutrality is essential to foster mutual respect and understanding in this world of divided religious sensibilities and religious fundamentalisms? Some even suggest that any idea of promoting the possibility of a Christian university is tantamount to a perversion of the true intention of a university, namely to encourage free thought. The assumption in this case is that tradition of any kind is inimical to free enquiry.[10] Indeed, the search for truth as evidenced in the modern university is one dogged by the legacy of the Enlightenment and a utilitarian attitude to knowledge, reflected in methodologies that are there to provide rules and systems of analysis.

II. John Henry Newman's Vision for Higher Education

The seeds for many of the developments we see today toward squeezing out religious traditions from the academe have a long history and were apparent to Cardinal John Henry Newman,

8 Gavin D'Costa, "On Theology's Babylonian Captivity within the Secular University," in Jeff Astley, Leslie Francis, John Sullivan and Andrew Walker, eds., *The Idea of a Christian University: Essays in Theology and Higher Education* (Carlisle: Paternoster Press, 2004), 183–189, citations 186–189.

9 Walter Brueggemann, "Slow Wisdom as a Sub-Version of Reality," this volume.

10 Elmer John Thiessen, "Objections to the Idea of a Christian University," in Astley et al., *The Idea of a Christian University*, 35–55.

writing in the middle of the nineteenth century (1852, 1858), at just about the same time Charles Darwin was penning his *Origin of Species* (1859), a work whose influence continues to reverberate even outside the discipline of biology. John Newman's work is perhaps less well known and appreciated by the public in the aftermath of the celebrations of Charles Darwin's significance, reaching their zenith in the anniversary year of 2009. Arguably it is Darwin, rather than Newman, who has most influenced the way educational practice has played out; for even though he did not support the new atheism currently in vogue, he set in motion questions about the status of the human being and faith in God, both aspects that Newman took for granted as essential for a rounded education. It may be for this reason that Frank Turner characterizes Newman's *Idea of a University* as "a voice from an academic time warp."[11] But important insights emerge for current concerns when this text is viewed in its historical context. Newman lived at a time when individualism was coming to the fore, and epistemic narrowness and simplicity replaced former, broader ways of thinking.[12] The dramatic advances in science that began in the seventeenth century were beginning to be felt in the public domain, and alongside this, an aping of the epistemology of science throughout the university environment as a whole, which is what I mean in using the term academe.

Newman believed, however, that there was some worth in scientific knowing as a form of intellectual training, which he described in terms of *notional* apprehension; that is, apprehension that is deductive, scientific, and logically conclusive. However, he also argued for *real* apprehension—knowing from a variety of factors through a collection of what he terms *weak evidences*. These

11 Frank M. Turner, "Newman's University and Ours," in *The Idea of a University*, ed. Turner (New Haven: Yale University Press, 1996), 284.

12 For a discussion of his work see Denis Robinson, "*Sedes Sapientiae*: Newman, Truth and the Christian University," in Astley et al., *The Idea of a Christian University*, 75–97.

included notions, images, historical occurrences, and emotions. The illative sense constructs knowledge through *practice*, so that there is a "going round an object, by the comparison, the combination, the mutual correction, the continual adaptation of many partial notions, by the employment, concentration and joint action of many faculties and exercises of the mind."[13] Hence, for real apprehension there needs to be a greater sensitivity to the complexity of truth. Newman believed that if we oversimplify, we fail in imagination, for we are not recognizing the truth that emerges out of daily activity. John Sullivan puts this well when he notes that "His approach to education in general and to educating faith in particular is engaged, experiential and imaginative; it is concrete, rather than abstract; it is very much living and personal knowledge that he promotes."[14]

The essence of ideology, and indeed, for Newman, heresy, is a failure to see tensions embedded in truths that are not necessarily resolvable. Such a view also echoes the thoughts of modern contemporary theologians, such as Emeritus Professor of philosophical theology Nicholas Lash, who claims that univocal thinking has effectively shut out other imaginative ways of knowing.[15] A similar controlling mind-set relates to what Walter Brueggemann had in mind in contrasting the fast wisdom and slow wisdom alluded to above. While Lash criticized the sciences for this type of thinking, I do not believe that such a criticism can simply be confined to the sciences, or that all contemporary sciences necessarily are *always* associated with such thinking. One could argue that univocal

13 J. Newman, *The Idea of the University* (London: Longmans, Green and Co, 1852), 152.

14 John Sullivan, "Newman's Circle of Knowledge and Curriculum Wholeness in *The Idea of the University*," in *The Reception of Newman*, ed. Frederick D. Aquino and Benjamin J. King (Oxford: Oxford University Press, 2015), 95–113. I am grateful to John Sullivan for allowing me to read a copy of his chapter before this book was published.

15 Nicholas Lash, *The Beginning and the End of Religion* (Cambridge: Cambridge University Press, 1996), 79.

thinking is characteristic of those who might be termed religious ultra-conservatives, who hold to creationism as a valid explanation of the origin of the universe and all life forms, for example.[16] The point is that Newman believed passionately in the proper training of one's mind, whatever the source, and he understood that excellence in intellectual training was hard to achieve.[17] Like contemporary philosophers such as Mary Midgley, Newman recognized there was a difference between education and simple acquisition of information. Midgley, writing in a contemporary context, is alert to the specialization and fragmentation that has taken place in different areas of knowledge, leaving behind the more holistic, but rigorous approach that Newman argued was so important.[18]

16   I have to use my words carefully here. In the UK such a position is often called "fundamentalist," but this is distinguished clearly from "evangelical." The former only reflects an entrenched position on creationism that advocates a young earth and the Genesis account as a literal "scientific" truth, especially in mirror reaction to the new atheism. There is insufficient space to discuss this in the context of this chapter, but it is taken up by John Haldane in "Wise and Otherwise," his chapter in this volume. Evangelicals are those, by contrast, who although they have a firm faith perspective in core areas, are open to knowledge from science, including evolutionary science, even if they are critical of the way science can become scientism. My own theological training in the 1980s began in an evangelical context, at Regents College, Vancouver, while I was a postdoctoral fellow in botany at the University of British Columbia.

17   Ian Ker believes that much of Newman's discussion in his *Idea of a University* is hyperbole and reflects the character of the Victorian age. What Newman seemed most concerned to promote was a liberal education, but this was not necessarily constricted to the *liberal arts* education. However, it seems to me that Newman was rather more alert to some of the dangers in *constricting* that training to scientific disciplines than Ker allows for in his analysis. See Ian Ker, *The Achievement of John Henry Newman* (London: Collins, 1991), 1–34.

18   Mary Midgley, *Wisdom, Information, and Wonder: What is Knowledge For?* (London: Routledge, 1991).

Newman also compared education to the nature of divine reality, so that the more one knows, the more one realizes that one does not know. The common search for truth links education with religion in an intimate way, as recognized by Pope John Paul II in *Ex Cordiae Ecclesia*, a document that sets out the theoretical and practical basis for the apostolic constitution of Catholic universities.[19] Such a way of knowing that is *also* informed by practices can be of service to the public good because it is influenced by a more rounded approach to truth. Newman believed that the only authentic university is also Christian because he believed that knowledge of God was necessary for complete learning. This is a different way of reasoning than that common among utilitarian thinkers, who view learning as useful only if strictly practical. Following the rise of experimental science in the seventeenth century, the idea that knowledge of the natural world could be gained through construction became dominant over the more contemplative forms of knowing in earlier centuries.[20] The constructive scientific knowledge base tends to be monocular. Instead, for Newman, the task of a university is purposefully to *complicate* the process by introducing convolution of learning that belies simple conveyance of information and techné.[21] At the same time he resisted eliding education with acquisition of limited or superficial knowledge across a range of disciplines; what is required is approaching the topics at hand with intellectual

---

19 John Henry Newman's *Idea of a University* is cited in this document and is one of the very few sources other than those deriving directly from the official Magisterium. John Sullivan also notes the significance of this source for defining the shape of Catholic higher education. See Pope John Paul II, *Ex Corde Ecclesiae*, http://www.vatican.va/holy_father/john_paul_ii/apost_constitutions/documents/hf_jp-ii_apc_15081990_ex-corde-ecclesiae_en.html, accessed January 30, 2015.

20 For a discussion see A. Funkenstein, *Theology and the Scientific Imagination*, (Princeton, NJ: Princeton University Press, 1986), 12; 297ff.

21 Robinson, "*Sedes Sapientiae*," 89.

rigor and the power to discriminate and assess the real value of things.[22]

Universities are, instead, to become in this way "seats of wisdom," such that they encourage a rigorous and multidisciplinary approach that encourages new insights to emerge in a community of learning. By multidisciplinary, I mean a focused attention on a *given complex topic* from different subject domains, and gathering together scholars from different disciplines in order to address issues that could not be answered easily from one perspective alone. John Sullivan describes this in terms of Newman's "circle of knowledge," the need for a *range* of disciplines in university education thus contributing to what might be termed "curriculum wholeness." Jane Rupert has also recognized the significance of Newman's riposte to epistemic narrowness in his requirement for a unified, comprehensive, and interconnected university education.[23] Pope John Paul II follows much the same idea in arguing for interdisciplinary studies, where science gains when "knowledge is joined to conscience" and "interaction with these other disciplines and their discoveries enriches theology, offering it a better understanding of the world today, and making theological research more relevant to current needs."[24] Philosophy in Newman's vision for university education played an architectonic role in highlighting the scope and limitations of each discipline. Newman was ahead of his time in this respect, in that such an approach is also one that some universities are actively experimenting with at the moment, drawing in faculty from different disciplines, including philosophical perspectives around one particular problematic topic.[25] Greater cultural awareness of globalization,

---

22 Ker, *The Achievement*, 14–15.

23 Jane Rupert, *John Henry Newman on the Nature of the Mind* (Lanham: Lexington Books, 2011).

24 Pope John Paul II, *Ex Corde Eccleisae*, para 18, para 19.

25 Stanley Hauerwas believes that the specialization of philosophy means that it can no longer take the kind of architectonic role that it once had in Newman's time, but that theology can now fill this gap. I suggest that retrieving ancient methods of philosophy can also be

arguably, forces universities to recognize the need for multidisciplinary perspectives, be it on areas such as sustainability, global health, or peace studies. The creation of numerous multidisciplinary institutes and graduate programs that cross subject domains once kept in watertight compartments at the University of Notre Dame, where I now teach, shows an openness to such a way of educating and researching. Such practices are, however, generally far slower to catch on in the UK, for while combined honors programs have been in place for some time, encouraging students to *integrate* such studies around specific problems or issues is far more challenging.

Newman did recognize that some universities would be specialized, and realized that not all universities could teach all possible subjects, but he argued that the ideal of universality should prevail, rather than some subjects being excluded as a matter of principle. Indeed, according to this model, interdisciplinary study—that is, study that is deliberately seeking to incorporate insights from different disciplinary areas—is not simply a good idea or a particular educational philosophy, but is *essential* in order to promote well-rounded students. Perhaps more important for Newman, education is not just a passive reception of knowledge, but a way of life, so that "universities inspire learners not to knowledge as a goal, but to the wisdom that a life of learning instills."[26] He also believed that knowledge ceases to be knowledge in so far as it tends more and more to the particular that is isolated from insight coming from broader patterns of thought and intellectual inquiry fostered in a community of students and teachers.

How different from the contemporary trend toward fragmentation in which university departments urge greater specialization in research as a way of attracting greater recognition of the "expert," especially in the public sphere![27] Such developments exist

useful, whether mediated through theology or not. Stanley Hauerwas, *The State of the University* (Oxford: Blackwell/Wiley, 2007), 23.

26 Robinson, "*Sedes Sapientiae*," 93.

27 See comment on this aspect in Deane-Drummond, Grove White and Szerszynski, "Genetically Modified Theology," 24–25.

somewhat in tension with the much slower growth in multidisciplinary approaches. In the UK context, the old Research Assessment Exercise (RAE), which gave credit for the most specialized and focused research supposedly deemed "world class" because it was unique in its field, has been charged with irrelevance by the new RAE scheme that asks, in addition, for clear evidence of impact. This new scheme seems equally flawed, but in a different way. I know colleagues who are considering sending out questionnaires following their delivery of conference papers as a way of providing concrete evidence that the audience changes in response to their ideas! While some universities may be succumbing to the research agenda in the way that Anthony Kronman suggests,[28] it is important to know precisely how that agenda is shaped, for it impacts the lives of those teaching in universities in important ways. Indeed, in the UK context, while some universities have their agenda shaped by research due to the considerable financial stakes and dependence on such funding for faculty positions, other institutions, like Chester University, perceive their role as primarily one of education, with research serving a secondary role that does not, at least for the most part, create dependency in terms of academic staff employment.

But what might the goal of that education be? It is certainly not simply to train in a particular profession, even a scientific research one, or to provide theoretical tools that will be useful in later practices. Rather, as Alasdair MacIntyre suggests, following Newman, "It is to transform their minds so that the student becomes a different kind of individual, one able to engage fruitfully in conversation and debate, one who has a capacity for exercising judgment, for bringing insights and arguments from a variety of disciplines to bear on particular complex issues."[29] But such prudential reasoning

28 Anthony Kronman, "Wisdom in the Age of the Research Ideal," this volume.
29 Alasdair MacIntyre, *God, Philosophy, Universities: A Selective History of the Catholic Philosophical Tradition* (Lanham, MD: Rowman & Littlefield, 2009), 147.

is not enough, because, following Aquinas, the exercise of prudence requires *moral* virtues as well.

Newman therefore acknowledged the importance of the perfection of the intellect, but this was not enough, for it could masquerade as portraying good character simply by its distaste of evil, rather than anything more profound. The difference between moral judgments and aesthetic judgments becomes particularly important in distinguishing between the kind of education that Newman had in mind and what might be termed purely secular education.[30] Aesthetic judgments are concerned with wider issues, but have their own internal judgments for their standard. Conscience, on the other hand, is concerned with self, and refers to a higher standard.[31] To describe the difference between purely intellectual education and what might be termed formation of an individual comes close to stating an argument for the place of theological wisdom in a university setting.

III. Why Might We Need Theological Wisdom?

For Newman, university life should rely on close cooperation between people, for it needs to reflect the collected community wisdom of those from different subject areas, experiences, and levels of education. Although he arguably neglected the importance of research,[32] finding ways of adjudicating the balance between

30 See discussion in MacIntyre, *God, Philosophy, Universities*, 149.

31 In the Roman Catholic tradition conscience is both individual, prompted by an inner sense of the voice of the Holy Spirit, and exists in relation to a wider community standard; in traditional thought this is represented by the official Magisterium.

32 See opening remarks in Sullivan, "Newman's Circle of Knowledge," 95–113. Of course, this also depends on what is meant by research. Newman's holistic approach was one that was highly integrative, but that in itself was a creative enterprise, and, as Sullivan suggests, "in his writings we see intermingled and integrated the interplay of memory, habit, active and critical thinking, prayer, imagination, feeling, belonging, the voice of conscience, our aesthetic sense, the mysterious

research and education in a university context is fraught with difficulties. It is hardly surprising that in the face of such pressures, a dualistic view is becoming more popular in the UK, with some arguing that a university can be committed to teaching or research, but never both.[33] The mix of research and education, however, is part of what might be termed the vocation of the university as an institution. Pope John Paul II refers to this as premised on a common love of knowledge, a principle which can equally apply to those universities who are not in the Roman Catholic tradition.[34] David Ford also makes the case for strengthening the links between research and teaching in a modern university context, and he sees this as an expression of wisdom.[35]

workings of grace and the part played by theology and doctrine and the church, plus the power of witness."

33 This also seemed to be the position advocated by John Haldane in his "Wise and Otherwise," this volume. While I can understand the pressure towards such a view, the opposite positions that can be held—namely, that research is (a) inimical to effective teaching, or (b) necessary for good teaching, both seem to me to be mistaken. Scholarship, understood as "low-level" research on a topic that does not include academic writing may be sufficient for most courses at degree level, but research is what inspires and drives many academics in their search for the truth. Students learn best when they are mentored by good, passionate teachers, and that passion is often ignited by research. Of course, where research becomes damaging to education is when those undertaking that research find themselves resentful of the demands of education, or those primarily committed to education are forced against their will to engage in research—the publish or perish mentality. But that does not mean research should be divorced from education; rather, it should be used as a spur to more effective communication with students by giving them insights from firsthand experience into the very human processes of discovery in science or developing an argument in the humanities.

34 Pope John Paul II, *Ex Corde Eccleisae*, para 1.

35 David Ford, *Christian Wisdom* (Cambridge: Cambridge University Press, 2007), 316–318.

But what if God is also the fount of wisdom, as Newman claims? The question that concerns us here is how the tradition of wisdom might inform the ethos of higher education. I suggest that wisdom does have something useful to say in debates about the role of the university today. Indeed, theologian David Ford identifies the whole task of theology as an exercise in or, perhaps more accurately, a cry for wisdom.[36] The fact that theology has continued to survive in spite of the pressures that I discussed earlier shows an inner resilience that emerges from the way many theologians perceive their academic work as a vocational task. Indeed, theological reflection needs to respond to the challenge of modernity and address its concerns without capitulating to its epistemological assumptions. David Ford's survey of the way theology has responded in the twentieth century shows that theological creativity is very much alive and well. But what specific contribution might it make to an educational ethos of the academe?

In the first place, theological wisdom's primary educational base is in the context of family and community. This way of learning was *practical* and *contextual* long before theologies bearing such a name came to the fore, often in reaction to more theoretical doctrinal discussions that seemed far too detached from ordinary life. This *praxis,* or theory informed by practices, is very different from utilitarian methods that simply emphasize usefulness for its own sake and as a means of control, detached from other forms of knowing and contemplation. If we apply this to the university with Newman, then, we can say that the context of students' living and community life is just as important as what they learn.

Second, theological wisdom is expressed in the Hebrew Bible

36 David Ford, *The Future of Christian Theology,* Blackwell Manifestos (Oxford: Wiley/Blackwell, 2011), 1–22. Ford also discusses the relationship between higher education and theology in his earlier book, David Ford, *Christian Wisdom,* 304–349. Here he uses the foundation of the University of Berlin (Humboldt) in 1810 as a paradigm of multidisciplinary conversation that he argues should inform the heart of university life.

in feminine categories.[37] Christian theology has been dogged in its history by interpretations that are influenced by patriarchal societies and assumptions. Catherine Keller, a leading feminist theologian, has drawn on the idea of *emancipatory wisdom* as that which best describes the future of theology in the university.[38] It is wisdom that can straddle the world of the academic and ecclesial communities to which theology must give an account of itself. For Keller, wisdom "at least as practiced in the indigenous and biblical traditions, is irredeemably implicated in the sensuous, the communal, the experiential, the metanoic, the unpredictable, the imaginal, the practical."[39] Her use of "metanoic" here is significant; it means being capable of changing hearts, from *metanoia,* change of heart. Such a view echoes the more traditional emphasis on the mystical goal of the religious life, where, as in Augustine, the heart is restless until it rests in God. This differs significantly from the coercive control of matter by mind, which dominates the agenda of modernity. For Keller it takes time to "let things become" and includes the social as well as an awareness of the importance of place.

Third, therefore, theological wisdom is not individualistic, but operates from within the social context, and reaches out even to the natural world, in a manner reminiscent of the work of environmentalist and educator Wendell Berry.[40] The importance of being

---

37 I am confining my discussion of wisdom to Christian theology, but this should not be taken to imply that I think other religions have little to offer debates on wisdom. Indeed, wisdom as a common motif can be a means through which different religious traditions can share their distinctive insights. I focus here on arguably the most dominant religious tradition in the Western world in order to show what insights this tradition might have on the university.

38 C. Keller, "Towards an Emancipatory Wisdom," in D. R. Griffin and J. C. Hough, eds., *Theology and the University: Essays in Honor of John B. Cobb, Jr.* (Albany: State University of New York Press, 1991), 125–147.

39 Keller, "Towards Emancipatory Wisdom," 143.

40 See, for example, Norman Wirzba, ed., *The Art of the Commonplace: Wendell Berry's Agrarian Essays* (Berkeley, CA: Counterpoint, 2003).

rooted in place is familiar to the wisdom writers; much wisdom literature is about day-to-day practical examples in one rooted community. The nomadic Israelites in the wilderness or, later, in exile still longed for the land of promise. The Celtic Christian traditions with which I am familiar pay special attention to place and ecology, and while reading ecological issues into Celtic wisdom is likely too simplistic, its capacity to speak to a contemporary audience comes from association and identification with place, just as much as its inherent beauty and poetry.[41] It has the capacity, therefore, of enlarging a person's horizons to think of those issues that are important, not just to the human community, but to the community of others in the world that God has created. Indeed, based on reflections on Proverbs 8, God could be said to create the world in love, but through wisdom.[42] Hence wisdom is a fundamental characteristic of the way God is perceived to create and sustain the world; here wisdom is perceived as a child at play, ever present with God at the dawn of existence.

Fourth, a theological voice is one that needs to be heard, for without it more extreme voices start to force their way into education's agenda. Newman was aware of this in his insistence that theology take its place in the circle of knowledge. If theology is stripped away from the university curriculum, then other disciplines will go beyond their limits to fill the vacuum.[43] Alasdair MacIntyre comments on this aspect of Newman's thought: where one science

41 For an excellent overview of the theological aspects of Celtic thought, see Tom O'Loughlin, *Celtic Theology: Humanity, World and God in Early Irish Writings* (London: Continuum, 2000).

42 A full discussion of this is outside the scope of this chapter. For more detail see C. Deane-Drummond, *Creation through Wisdom: Theology and the New Biology* (Edinburgh: T&T Clark, 2000).

43 As Sullivan points out, taking theology out of the curriculum is detrimental in that first it assumes that theology has no worthwhile knowledge, and second it mutilates the circle of knowledge by providing opportunities for disciplines to exceed their limits. Sullivan, "Newman's Circle of Knowledge," 95–113.

is removed another comes to fill the void, so that economics attempts competency in ethics, or science in theology.[44] More contemporary expressions of this take the form of scientism and its opposite theological reaction in creationist science. Such a worrying trend is only too apparent in the way that those wishing to promote creationist science have begun creeping their way into the school curriculum in the United Kingdom. While creationist science's voice has become rather more sophisticated through the notion of Intelligent Design, it still seeks to provide an ideological alternative to Darwinian accounts. It is hardly surprising that, as far as I am aware, most state universities in the United States want to exclude theology from the university curriculum. Many thoughtful academics want to keep theology out of higher education; even sophisticated and well-respected geneticists such as Steve Jones seem to elide creationism and a theology of creation.[45] Yet, is it not for this *very reason* that such counter-reactions have found their force? For if people are inculcated into utilitarian methods of learning and thinking at universities, where distorted versions of Darwinism take the form of new atheism, then a culture that is generally religious will sense some disorientation and be more inclined to an equally narrow and ill-informed reaction to that scientism. In other words, a narrowing of epistemology through a secularist agenda (as that expressed in university education) leads to a counter reaction that is, ironically, a reflection of such narrowness expressed in religious terms. Hence the importance of a rich understanding of theological wisdom, which will discourage such retreats into apparently safe havens and is excluded from the worst excesses of those particular forms of scientific knowing that subsequently become expressed in narrow public policies and practices.

44 A. MacIntyre, *God, Philosophy, Universities*, 146.
45 This was evident in a public lecture "Why Evolution is Right and Creationism is Wrong" that he gave at the Cheshire Literature Festival, speaking at the University of Chester on October 11, 2006. See also, S. Jones, *In the Blood: God, Genes and Destiny* (Harper Collins, 1997).

Fifth, and more radical perhaps, the New Testament theological wisdom finds expression through a paradox of suffering, rather than a celebration of human wisdom, in the wisdom of the cross.[46] While not doing away with the human wisdom of the sages, the wisdom of the cross points to another way of being that makes most sense in the context of the Christian community. Yet could the wisdom of the cross have wider relevance? Can we say, with Pope John Paul II, that the wisdom coming from Christ enables a person to find ultimate reality, "that Wisdom without which the future of the world would be in danger"?[47] Certainly, it shows that a Christian image of God is one on the side of those who are suffering and in pain. One of the important tasks of the university is to be pastoral and open to those with special needs; students do not achieve in a vacuum, but are enabled to do so through lived experiences. If these lived experiences are too traumatic, learning may suffer, at least temporarily. I witnessed numerous examples of this in my experience at the University of Chester, which opened its doors to students of all backgrounds in order to enable wider access to higher education. It is here that a university needs to include not just a curricula program, but also provide for pastoral needs of its students through adequate counseling and chaplaincy provision.

Discussion of the wisdom of the cross in the epistle to the Corinthians is also set in the context of an early Christian community, where different groups were vying for authority according to different perceptions of philosophical or, more accurately, rhetorical wisdom. Instead of such rhetorical game playing, the author of the epistle encourages reflection on the wisdom of the cross. Such wisdom speaks of the need for humility, rather than jockeying for positions of power through clever forms of speech. Is such a goal realistic in a university context? What would the shape of university management be like if such an approach was adopted by vice chancellors and college presidents?

---

46 The first letter of Paul to the Corinthians; for example, especially 1 Cor. 1:8–2:5.

47 Pope John Paul II, *Ex Corde Ecclesia*, para 4.

IV. Why Might We Need Practical Wisdom?

The medieval theologian Thomas Aquinas distinguished between the intellectual virtues of speculative reason and those of practical reason. The intellectual virtues of speculative reason included understanding, science, and wisdom, where wisdom is the appreciation of the fundamental causes of everything and the connections between them, including God. The practical virtues, on the other hand, included art and prudence, or practical wisdom.[48] Prudence, in the classical sense, includes deliberation, judgment, and action. How might prudence inform an institution such as a university? In the first place, prudence is both individual and political. Hence it has a social dimension, so there is a need not just to encourage students to think prudentially, but to apply prudence to forms of management and institutional structures as well. Yet, in a popular cast of mind, prudence is often portrayed as caution about taking risks, at least as applied to political decision making. The classical notion is so different that it is worth considering whether the term prudence should still be used in such a context.

Prudence, for the classics, has a number of different facets that are worth highlighting in this context. In the first place, it is sensitive to memory of the past; that is, it is conscious of what has gone before and has learned the lessons from this history. John Henry Newman's approach to university education has been largely ignored, at least in terms of practical application. An alternative style of university ethos compared with the current focus on utilitarian management is essential so that universities are enabled to become,

---

48   Aquinas distinguished wisdom, a virtue of speculative reason, from prudence, a virtue of practical reason, by naming wisdom as that which dealt specifically with theological matters, and prudence as that which dealt with human affairs. For his discussion of wisdom see Aquinas, *Summa Theologiae*, vol. 34, *Charity*, trans. R. J. Batten (London: Blackfriars, 1975), 2a2ae. For his discussion of prudence see Aquinas, *Summa Theologiae*, vol. 36, *Prudence*, trans. T. Gilby (London: Blackfriars, 1973).

as Newman suggested, "seats of wisdom." Alasdair MacIntyre argued in this vein when he suggested that there are three rival versions of moral inquiry, only one of which has served to inform the modern university, namely the one based on the Enlightenment project.[49] The second tradition that he identifies is what he terms the genealogy of Nietzsche, which leads to forms of postmodernity that seek to deconstruct all foundations for knowledge. If such a postmodern project were taken too literally, it is hard to imagine how universities might function.[50] The third form of inquiry he identifies is that of Thomas Aquinas, which he suggests provides a bridge between universal forms of disembodied reason found in the first Enlightenment project, and the second form that encourages relativism. Certainly, the Aristotelian tradition of prudence influences Aquinas, but I suggest that Aquinas's view goes even further than just providing a bridge between modern and postmodern views in the way that MacIntyre suggests. For Aquinas holds fast to the importance of theology in his construction; it is not simply an "add on," in the manner of grace being added to nature (as his position is sometimes portrayed in basic theology textbooks). Rather, Aquinas is sensitive to the importance of religious experience, even admitting toward the end of his life that his monumental treatise on theology was "like straw," following what seems to have been a mystical experience of God. Here he seems to be saying at the minimum that theological rational analysis needs to find its completion in a living experience of God.[51] There is in Aquinas, in

49 Alasdair MacIntyre, *Three Rival Versions of Moral Enquiry* (London: Duckworth, 1990).

50 A caveat for this view is that arguably Derrida's own view of endless questioning means that the university is still obliged to remember the older universal story in its questioning, rather than simply cast this to one side. See G. Loughlin, "The University without Question: John Henry Newman and Jacques Derrida on Faith in the University," in Astley, et al. (eds.), *The Idea of a Christian University*, 113–131.

51 See discussion in Josef Pieper, *The Silence of St. Thomas* (South Bend, IN: St. Augustine's Press, 1999). John Caputo argues that Thomas's

other words, a crucial sensitivity to the presence of God, a contemplative dimension, that MacIntyre does not seem to have taken sufficiently seriously. Prudence for Aquinas is not simply learned in the human community; it is also a gift of the Holy Spirit received by the grace of God. In addition, for Aquinas, prudence, along with the other cardinal virtues, presupposes the theological virtues of faith, hope, and charity.

Second, practical wisdom in Aquinas is conscious of what is the case in the present, and is open to being taught. This openness is an essential ingredient of all learning, at whatever level and whatever the final goal of such learning. Deliberation needs to include, therefore, consultation with others, both within and outside of individual disciplines. Furthermore, are such different academic disciplines open to being restructured? Theology, which Gavin D'Costa has described as being "in Babylonian captivity" by its aping of secular agendas, could arguably be the first to remember its lost wisdom and seek alternatives. While other disciplines might find it hard to extricate themselves from the specialism that seems to engender authority and funding, at least as a first move, different subject areas could seek to scrutinize the overall goals of their research and knowledge transfer programs. Practical wisdom is also able to make correct decisions in the face of the unexpected. If universities are to become those seats of wisdom, then they too will have something to say when unexpected events happen that need

comparison pointed to the *fulfillment* of theology in mysticism, rather than any sense of rejection of its worth. See John Caputo, *Heidegger and Aquinas: An Essay in Overcoming Metaphysics* (New York: Fordham University Press, 1982), 256. This is put beautifully in Pieper's analysis where a search for understanding the world opens up to mystery and unknowing, so that "the very element which makes [things] capable of being known, must necessarily be at the same time the reason why things are unfathomable" (Pieper, *Silence of St. Thomas*, 66). The point in the context of this lecture is that unless theological reflection recognizes the limitations of knowing, however sophisticated that theology might be, it ceases to carry weight.

public comment, as discussed in more detail in the final section below.

Third, practical wisdom combines both caution and foresight. Caution is awareness of where mistakes have been made in the past, and being able to adjust future policy in the light of those mistakes. Have universities really learned from their mistakes, or are they bent on ever more accumulative strategies, orientated to utilitarian goals? Can foresight enable universities to see into the future as to what different strategies might entail, and how each might be implemented? If universities continue to be led by market driven policies, then not only will the basis for learning be undermined—for some subjects will disappear as being unfashionable—but universities will become narrowed to centers for vocational training, and the curriculum adjusted to what is needed for a market economy. In this way, the university will no longer be a place where new questions are asked of society, but one where the values of society are simply reinforced.

What might an alternative vision include? In Aquinas, practical wisdom is wisdom oriented toward the good. Although there are philosophical debates about what this good might entail, a vision for the public good—that is, the good for the whole community—goes some way toward expressing what he intends. A Christian university would also wish this good to be grounded in an understanding of theological good. For Aquinas, this Divine Wisdom is reflected in practical terms through the Decalogue; that is, the Ten Commandments. Although detached from its origins, the legal structure that exists in Britain is also influenced by the Christian context in which it emerged. Yet universities need to seek not just to encourage their students to be law-abiding citizens (though certainly they can do this), but also to serve the communities in which they are placed.

V. Practical Wisdom In Service To The Public Good

In order to illustrate how practical wisdom fostered in a university setting might inform the public good, I am going to use one area of public discussion; namely, environmental concerns. What might a prudential approach, understood according to the classical tradition that I have been elaborating, have to say on these issues? While it is quite possible to understand prudence without any reference to Christian theology, I suggest that retrieving a classical and Thomistic notion of prudence, which acknowledges its links with Christian virtue, serves to provide a bridge between secular and religious aspects of human community that also helps serve the public good. In other words, we do not just need a bridge between modern and postmodern, which MacIntyre correctly identifies as one of the roles of virtue traditions, but also a bridge between secular and religious streams of human life.

I am illustrating how practical wisdom might be useful through the example of sustainability. This chapter will not attempt to provide specific evidence that sustainability and climate change are important global issues to consider. Sustainability is a subject that lends itself to a multidisciplinary approach, from physics, chemistry, geography, through to economics, social science, philosophy, anthropology, and theology. It is also, ironically perhaps, subject to captivity to the market in common with other ways of thinking, in that it can become a market commodity, merely serving to promote particular economic interests. An alternative that is particularly evident in climate change debates is that the scientific discussion takes over at the expense of wider cultural issues. But I suggest that contested questions around sustainability also allow for a theological dimension for a number of reasons.

In the first place, the religious aspects of sustainability concerns are often thought of by practical campaign conservation groups as simply a way to reinforce a sustainable agenda. If Christians are able to support sustainability because of their faith commitment, then, the argument goes, so much the better, for religious motivation will reinforce commitment. Religion is therefore brought into the discussion purely for pragmatic reasons. Yet in consultations on what sustainability might mean among conservation groups, which often include an account of future generations, little account has been taken of what Christian communities might actually have to say on sustainability and what sustainability might or must include.[52] This exclusion of Christian communities as having something worthwhile to say reflects, it seems to me, a lack of prudence or practical wisdom.

In addition, environments that are sustainable need to be places where we feel at home, engendering connectivity with the past. Does sustainability in its current definitions take into account this need for *memory*, which is another vital aspect of prudential reasoning? Ecologist and Anglican priest John Rodwell questions whether "the sustainability process knows how to handle the past at all."[53] There is, furthermore, a lack of appreciation in visions of a sustainable future as to whether justice has been done to the past, for the focus is on the needs of future generations, or of the more immediate ecological community. Yet the engagement with such concerns reveals the very real development which theology has undergone in responding to the pressures of modern and postmodern societies. With David Ford, I recognize that not only does theology speak into a given culture, but theology and religious studies as a field are transformed in a way that holds to serious intellectual inquiry in conversation with other disciplines and other religious traditions. Ford calls this "new theology and religious studies."[54] On one level theology is new, in that it is grounded in a new context, but the search for meaning, truth and intellectual honesty, and humility is the same today as it was when Aquinas struggled to make sense of the dominant science and philosophies of his time.

Finally, the importance of a religious voice in the public sphere is something that is now being recognized as important in order to deal with contested issues of social importance. This is particularly the case where science is beginning to impact the social sphere,

52 I am drawing here on the work of Rev. Professor John Rodwell and his M. B. Reckitt Lecture, "Forgetting the Land," delivered at Mirfield College, September 7, 2006. This was published as a journal article in *Studies in Christian Ethics* 21, no. 2 (2008): 268–286.
53 Rodwell, "Forgetting the Land."
54 Ford, *The Future of Christian Theology*, 150–154.

raising profound and difficult social questions. Even those philosophers who are wedded to modernist views recognize the importance of remembering religious traditions in areas of public importance. Jürgen Habermas, for example, admits to a significant role of religion:

> Christianity has functioned for the normative self-understanding of modernity as more than a mere precursor or catalyst. Egalitarian universalism, from which sprang the ideas of freedom and social solidarity, of an autonomous conduct of life and emancipation, of the individual morality of conscience, human rights, democracy, is the direct heir to the Judaic ethic of justice and the Christian ethic of love . . . . To this day there is no alternative to it.[55]

If even secular philosophers are now admitting to the vital importance of remembering modernity's debt to religious traditions and its likely significance in the public domain, then it is not out of keeping to argue for a similar shift in provision for university education.

VI. Conclusions

I suggest that a religious dimension to public debate is forgotten at our peril. Universities are subject to this same form of forgetting—an amnesia that reflects the loss of connection with their historical foundation. I have argued that we can learn some important lessons about the possible shape of university education by returning to the work of John Henry Newman. He lived at a time when knowledge was becoming ever more narrow in its focus, excluding what once had been presupposed as a good. His writing on the concept

55 Jürgen Habermas, *Time of Transitions*, Ciaran Cronin and Max Pensky, eds., trans. Ciaran Cronin and Max Pensky (Cambridge: Polity, 2006), 150–151.

of a Christian university is not simply a defense of the existence of such institutions. Rather, I suggest that his thinking has wider application, and can contribute to the construction of an overall shape for all university education. Not all universities will have the same agenda, but all can be challenged to encourage in their students more holistic ways of learning. This includes a seeking of wisdom that is multidimensional in its scope.

I have also argued that, while theological wisdom has become a voice that is often marginalized and excluded from university educational agendas, this exclusion is a mistake; for within theology there are resources that can make a valuable contribution to re-envisioning an agenda for higher education. In particular, this agenda needs to be emancipatory, but such emancipatory knowing is one that is practical as well as multifaceted. Newman's vision of cooperation comes to the fore here, for without mutual respect for the contribution of different disciplines (as in multidisciplinary approaches to education and research), universities soon start to imitate that divided community of Corinth where each group vied for its own superiority.[56] Instead, proper account needs to be made of the common good, and how to reach this goal in the context of the local and wider community. While what that good might mean will be much more contested now—especially in Western pluralistic societies—compared to the medieval idealized view, at least some sense of a common goal is important in opening up universities to agendas wider than the narrowly conceived educational one.

Thomas Aquinas's brilliance in synthesizing the thought of Aristotle with Augustine still has relevance today, especially in his discussion of practical wisdom or prudence. Universities too need to be places where synthetic knowledge is encouraged, especially if they are to form seeds for alternative ways of thinking that resist monocularity. Public debates are too often ill informed, not only about science, which is perhaps recognized, but also about the place of religious understanding, as illustrated through discussions of sus-

---

56 I am referring here to the portrayal of this community by the apostle Paul in his first letter to the Corinthians.

tainability. Universities need, therefore, to be places that can inform public opinion so that more accurate representation takes place. In this way, a public that is better informed than would otherwise be the case will serve to help shape government policy. Moreover, universities need to be places that instill in their students the love of learning that goes far deeper than simple success at examinations. For this kind of instilled wisdom does not just offer skills that are "transferable," but helps to foster *citizen virtues*, those which enable active and full responsibility, not just in family life, but in the public sphere as well.

Evolution, Education, and Wisdom
John Haldane

I. Introduction

In this essay I shall be concerned with two themes: the place of the cultivation of wisdom within higher education, particularly but not exclusively within the study of the humanities; and the threat to such studies posed by scientism and by the application of certain ideas derived from evolutionary theory. This will strike some readers as a surprising and perhaps provocative combination of subjects; but I hope it will become clear why I have chosen to address these issues and to conjoin them.

II. Science and Scientism

Viewed from a nineteenth-century perspective, there is little in the details of contemporary political life that would seem special. Tensions between great powers, ethnic and religious divisions, trade rivalries, economic recessions, currency crises, civil unrest, and so on, are all part of the fabric of the modern world. Social life in the West has been marked by the dissolution of families and communities into voluntary and market associations of individuals; but while that was a distinctive feature of the twentieth century and has extended into the twenty-first, it is a continuation of trends well-established through industrialization and urbanization in previous times.

The issues of pure and applied science are somewhat different. For whatever future advances may serve to diminish the achievements of the present age, it is clear that the twentieth century was one of remarkable and ever-accelerating scientific and technological development, and that the range, extent, and forms of this development were largely unimaginable in the nineteenth century.

Because of this, science has come to enjoy enormous prestige and to be widely viewed as the primary source of concepts and theories sufficient to describe and explain all of reality, including human beings. An older Baconian conception of science regarded it as the philosophically unassuming, phenomena-identifying, hypothesis-formulating study of the material composition and causal structure of nature. But that has been replaced by a view of science as queen of the philosophies, bearing down upon metaphysics and theology—possibly to press them into new vital forms, but more likely to crush the life out of them. A testament to this new view is found in Stephen Hawking's recent book, *The Grand Design*, in which he writes:

> [H]uman beings are a curious species. We wonder, we seek answers . . . . How can we understand the world in which we find ourselves? How does the universe behave? What is the nature of reality? . . . Traditionally these are questions for philosophy, but philosophy is dead. Philosophy has not kept up with modern developments in science, particularly physics, [and] scientists have become the bearers of the torch of discovery in our quest for knowledge.[1]

Hawking's concern is with cosmological issues, but if we turn to questions about human nature and moral consciousness it is not hard to find prominent declarations that traditional philosophical approaches have failed and that the lead must now be taken by innovative sciences. The following, for example, comes from the Introduction to Patricia Churchland's recent book (subtitled) *What Neuroscience Tells Us About Morality*:

1 Stephen Hawking (and Leonard Mlodinow), *The Grand Design* (New York: Bantam, 2010), 5. I discuss these claims of Hawking in "Philosophy Lives," *First Things* (January 2011) 43–46.

The phenomenon of moral values, *hitherto* so puzzling, is *now* less so. Not entirely clear, just less puzzling. By drawing on converging new data from neuroscience, evolutionary biology, experimental psychology and genetics, and *given a philosophical framework consilient with those data*, we can *now* meaningfully approach the question of where values come from.[2] [my emphasis]

Seen in these ways, our age is one of scientific thought that is less in dialogue with, than in judgment upon, philosophical, ethical and religious habits of mind. It should be clear that this presents a serious challenge to traditional humanism, in the sense that it interprets significance and value from the point of view of phenomenologically or reflectively accessible human needs, interests, sensibilities, and practices; in other words, from the viewpoint of lived human experience. For much of the twentieth century, the focus of humanistic concern regarding science was the potential of its applications to destroy human life through biochemical and nuclear warfare. More recently, however, the focus of attention has shifted somewhat from the pros and cons of instrumental technology to the potential for science to change the way we think about human beings and, indeed, to change their very nature by chemical, genetic, and surgical interventions.

III. Challenges Posed By Evolutionary Theories

I do not know who first suggested a connection between theories of evolution and the practice of education; but insofar as the former bears upon the issue of human origins and nature, and the latter is concerned with human development, the idea that there are relevant connections must have occurred to many. An early example is that of Herbert Spencer who, in 1857, published an essay entitled

2   Patricia S. Churchland, *Braintrust: What Neuroscience Tells Us about Morality* (Princeton, NJ: Princeton University Press, 2011), 3.

"Progress: its Law and Cause"[3] and five years later developed its central ideas under the title *First Principles of a New System of Philosophy*. Between these dates came the publication of Darwin's *The Origin of Species*, which Spencer immediately read; yet, while his system is often referred to as "social Darwinism," it is quite different in fundamental respects.

First, under the influence of German philosophical and scientific theories (mediated in part by the poet Coleridge), Spencer thought of the history of life and of the universe more generally, in progressive directional terms, as proceeding toward a state of complex equilibrium. Second, he was a Lamarkian, supposing that acquired characteristics developed in use may be passed on to offspring (and unused ones lost to the species). These characteristics include bodily organs and the faculties that they serve. The human faculties that especially came to interest Spencer are those involved in social development through the acquisition of knowledge—both *consciously* in the individual, and *unconsciously* as the inherited experience of specific populations.

From this "evolutionary" theory, Spencer drew somewhat ambiguous conclusions so far as education is concerned. Progress depends upon knowledge and the development of knowledge depends upon human beings, individually and socially, recognizing the consequences of their behavior. From that point of view, so long as education focuses upon direct, experienced connections between conduct and outcome, it is advantageous. On the other hand, if it were to bypass these vital natural links it would be counter-progressive, and hence counter-evolutionary. In these terms one might speak of a Spencerian doctrine: contributing to evolution is the

3   *Westminster Review* 67 (1857): 445–485. Spencer was a member of the English radical movement out of which the *Review* had been founded three decades earlier by Jeremy Bentham. Its purpose was to provide a forum for new thought on matters relating to human advancement and it was there that the term "Darwinism" was first coined by Thomas Huxley in his review of the *Origin of Species*, 1860, 541–570.

criterion of educational adequacy. Whatever the status of its theoretical assumptions, however, such a doctrine is philosophically and ethically problematic in that it overlooks, or sets aside the idea that the value of education is intrinsic to it. In particular, coming to understand a concept, or a theory, or a practice, constitutes one of the goods of human life quite apart from the question of whether it provides utilitarian benefit. In short, the Spencerian view instrumentalizes education, and does so on a dubious account of the end toward which it ought to be directed.

Spencer's philosophical concerns have no direct relationship with the later and more familiar connection between evolution and education; namely, that involved in the controversies surrounding the teaching of evolutionary theories in American schools. The most famous of these disputes arose from John Scopes's use of George William Hunter's 1914 textbook *Civic Biology*[4] in defiance of Tennessee legislation prohibiting public universities and public schools from teaching "any theory that denies the Story of the Divine Creation of man as taught in the Bible and teach[ing] instead that man has descended from a lower order of animals."[5] The debates around this issue are well known and generally unedifying, but they contributed to a persistent impression that theories of evolution are necessarily at odds with a religious understanding of human beings. Much work has gone into showing that this is not so; but if it is facile to suggest that evolution negates the idea of divine creation, it is also facile to suppose that there may be no tension between naturalistic theories of human origins and spiritual accounts of human nature—and hence no tension between the teaching of certain kinds of evolutionary theories and certain kinds of religious and philosophical education.

---

4   George William Hunter, *A Civic Biology: Presented in Problems* (New York: American Book Co., 1914).
5   *Tennessee Evolution Statutes* (Nashville: State of Tennessee, 1925), Chapter 27, House Bill No. 185; repealed in 1967.

IV. From Darwin to Dhobzanski

The first major scientific challenge to traditional ideas of humanity came in 1871 with the publication of Darwin's speculations in *The Descent of Man*. There he applied the evolutionary theory presented in *The Origin of Species* to the case of human beings, and on that basis, was led to write that "the difference in mind between man and the higher animals, great as it is, certainly is one of degree and not of kind."[6] Prior to this the prevailing idea, which had originated in antiquity with the pre-Socratics and constituted philosophical orthodoxy through the Late-Hellenic, Medieval, Renaissance, and Enlightenment periods, was of a hierarchy of species with *Homo sapiens* set apart from the rest of nature by its capacity for reason and moral consciousness. Darwin himself observed that ""No one supposes that one of the lower animals reflects whence he comes or whither he goes,—what is death or what is life, and so forth"[7] but, as indicated by his deliberate contrast between differences of "degree" and of "kind," he thought this was ultimately only a *quantitative* rather than a *qualitative* distinction.

The possibility that our moral and spiritual consciousness and our rationality, along with our upright posture and sparsity of body hair, might be the result of natural selection driving "descent with modification" from apes was deeply disturbing to the Victorians. In due course, though, various modes of accommodation between theology and evolution were arrived at, principally by religious parties (re)interpreting their claims in terms that rendered them compatible with scientific explanations of the operations of nature. Some reflective readers, however, saw the threat not only to theological anthropology but also to traditional *humanist* understandings, and they pointed to particular areas that seemed to resist

6   Charles Darwin, *The Descent of Man and Selection in Relation to Sex* (Princeton, NJ: Princeton University Press, 1981), 104; see ch. 3 and 4, "Comparison of the Mental Powers of Man and Lower Animals."

7   Darwin, *Descent of Man*, 62.

reduction. An anonymous reviewer of *The Descent*, writing in the *Edinburgh Review* in the same year as the book's publication (1871) pressed a charge that is still worthy of consideration. The reviewer writes:

> Mr. Darwin's theory of the growth of the moral sense and of the intellectual faculty is unsupported by any proof; and the very corner-stone of the hypothesis, that the human mind is identical in kind with that of the brutes, is a mere assumption opposed alike to experience and philosophy . . . . man's intellect and moral sense are now, as they ever were, inscrutable from the point of view offered by natural history; and only to be compre-hended from far higher considerations, to which, as a mere naturalist, Mr. Darwin has not attained.[8]

I shall return to this point, but before doing so I want to con-sider a general argument for scientific reductionism implied by a famous remark from a major twentieth-century disciple of Dar-win, the Russian geneticist Theodosius Dobzhansky. The saying, oft cited by evolutionary biologists, is that "Nothing in biology makes sense except in the light of evolution." This bold dictum formed the title of an article Dobzhansky published in 1973 in the *American Biology Teacher*. There he challenged biblical cre-ationism, opposing it with the idea of "a process that began some ten billion years ago and is still under way."[9] Interestingly, how-ever, he also claimed that far from evolution being incompatible with divine creation, it is its method. He did not, however, venture the further thought to which an advocate of theistic arguments from fine-tuning or natural regularity might be attracted—that

8   "Darwin on the Descent of Man," *The Edinburgh Review* 134 (July 1871): 195–235; 235.

9   Theodosius Dobzhansky, "Nothing in Biology Makes Sense Except in the Light of Evolution," *American Biology Teacher* 33 (March 1973): 125–129.

evolution only, or best, makes sense in the light of purposeful design.

One might wonder why Dobzhansky did not consider or even acknowledge the existence of such arguments. Ignorance of, or hostility to theological speculation can hardly be the answer since he was raised Russian Orthodox and described himself as religious. Indeed, these biographical facts are sometimes merged to suggest that he was a traditional theist, as for example by Stephen Jay Gould who described Dobzhansky as "the greatest evolutionist of our time and a lifelong Russian Orthodox" in his article, "Darwinism Defined."[10] In fact, however, Dobzhansky did not believe in a personal God, or in any transcendent creative source outside of nature. Rather, he seems to have identified creation with evolution itself. Immediately prior to the sentence I quoted earlier he writes: "I am a creationist and an evolutionist. Evolution is God's or Nature's method of creation," and he ends the article by commending Teilhard de Chardin's immanentism, citing a familiar passage from *The Phenomenon of Man*:

> [Evolution] is a general postulate to which all theories, all hypotheses, all systems must henceforth bow and which they must satisfy in order to be thinkable and true. Evolution is a light which illuminates all facts, a trajectory which all lines of thought must follow—this is what evolution is."[11]

The overall impression is of a kind of Spinozistic-cum-Hegelian, spiritualized evolutionism with man representing the emergence of self-awareness. Not only did Dobzhansky favor evolutionary theory as the best account of observed biological diversity and unity, he regarded it as fully comprehensive in scope and in explanatory role. As he wrote elsewhere:

10 Stephen Jay Gould, "Darwinism Defined: The Difference between Fact and Theory," *Discover* (January 8) 1987, 64–70.
11 Teilhard de Chardin, *The Phenomenon of Man* (New York: Harper and Row, 1965), 215.

Evolution comprises all the stages of the development of the universe: the cosmic, biological, and human or cultural developments. Attempts to restrict the concept of evolution to biology are gratuitous. Life is a product of the evolution of inorganic nature, and man is a product of the evolution of life.[12]

V. Making Sense, and a Transitive Fallacy

These remarks suggest and perhaps license a step-wise extension of Dobzhansky's original aphorism: *nothing in religion makes sense except in the light of psychology; nothing in psychology makes sense save in the light of biology; nothing in biology makes sense except in the light of evolution.* However, even assuming, for the moment, the truth of the individual clauses, it is not clear that one can simply conclude from their conjunction that nothing in religion makes sense save in the light of evolution.

Explanation is not in general a logically transitive relation. That nothing in David's behavior (sweating) made sense save in the light of Mary's presence, and that nothing in Mary's behavior (blushing) made sense save in the light of John's presence do not conjointly imply that nothing in David's behavior made sense save in the light of John's presence. What does make sense in each case may be restricted to that case: David's feeling for Mary and Mary's infatuation with John. One might, perhaps, say that John's presence was *per accidens* a cause of David's sweating, but it is not *per se* an explanation of it. Furthermore there are contextual assumptions about background facts that form part of the explanation, and not of what is to be explained, and these assumptions may vary in several dimensions reflecting various human interests, meanings, and values.

Making sense in the light of is an incomplete notion, and relevant specifications drawing upon features of religion, morality, psychology, biology, and evolutionary theory may yield no overall

12 Theodosius Dobzhansky, "Changing Man," *Science* 155, no. 3761 (January 1967): 409–415; 409.

explanatory relation between level-specific features of religion and of evolution respectively. Put less abstractly, even were it the case that moral experience or religious practice only made sense when seen psychologically as a form of social bonding, say, and social bonding only made sense when seen biologically in terms of common species membership, and that in turn only made sense when seen in terms of evolutionary history, it would not follow that the theory of speciation by natural selection makes sense of moral experience and religious practice—let alone "the only sense" there is to be made of them. In order for that to be so, the features in question would have to be of the same sort and appropriately linked, and to presume this would amount to a strong, and unwarranted, form of reductionism. Just to press home the point, consider additional clauses to the effect that speciation by natural selection only makes sense in the light of genetics, that in light of biochemistry, and that in light of physics. Anyone inclined to think that it follows, therefore, that nothing in morality or religion makes sense, save in the light of physics, needs to revisit the idea of *making sense.*

What then of the truth of the individual clauses? Dobzhansky's main claim was that two marked features of life on earth cannot be made sense of save in the light of evolutionary theory: first, biological diversity, amounting to several million species varying in size, structure, behavior, and habitat; and second, biological relatedness, as evidenced by widespread biological similarities at the level of anatomy and embryology, and the universal encoding of heredity at the biochemical level. Of themselves, these are compatible with a variety of explanations, but let me follow Dobzhansky and accept as their best explanation the assumption of common ancestry and diversification through variation, heritability, and natural selection. What of the further claim that natural evolution comprises human and cultural developments, including ethics and religion?

VI. Overlapping Magisteria

In an address to the Pontifical Academy of Sciences in 1996 entitled "On Evolution," Pope John Paul II reiterated the position affirmed by Pope Pius XII in his 1950 encyclical *Humani Generis* that "there is no conflict between evolution and the doctrine of faith."[13] Moreover, Pope John Paul II went further in acknowledging the explanatory power of evolutionary science to the extent of saying that "the theory of evolution is more than a hypothesis." The positions of the two popes are discussed in detail by Stephen Jay Gould in one of the last books he published: *Rocks of Ages: Science and Religion in the Fullness of Life.*[14] The main theme of this is the presentation and defense of the idea of non-overlapping magisteria ("NOMA"), according to which science is seen as explaining the material structure of the world, while religion addresses the subject of its (possible) meaning. Gould explains that he had originally assumed that John Paul's statement was "fully consistent with long-standing Roman Catholic support for NOMA," but on reading *Humani Generis,* came to see that there is a significant difference between the two papal documents and the attitudes animating them:

> Pius had grudgingly admitted evolution as a legitimate hypothesis that he regarded as only tentatively supported and potentially (as he clearly hoped) untrue. John Paul, nearly fifty years later, reaffirms the legitimacy of evolution under the NOMA principle, but then adds that additional data and theory have placed the factuality of evolution beyond reasonable doubt.[15]

13 John Paul II, "Message to the Pontifical Academy of Sciences: On Evolution," 22 October 1996.

14 Stephen Jay Gould, *Rocks of Ages: Science and Religion in the Fullness of Life* (New York: Ballantine, 1999), see 75–82. Following the British publication of *Rocks of Ages,* Gould, Hilary Rose, and I discussed the idea of whether or not religion and science are in competition at any point. This was in the BBC series *In Our Time* and the program can be heard at http://www.bbc.co.uk/programmes/p005479y.

15 Ibid., 82.

The spread of knowledge has made us less innocent than Darwin's contemporaries and our degree of intellectual pluralism and diversification means we are more used to compartmentalizing ideas and values. Nonetheless, like the author in the *Edinburgh Review* we too should feel challenged by current scientific enquiry into aspects of human nature and be aware that the reconciliation Gould recommends may not always be possible. Most theists, for example, are committed to the following beliefs:

1) the universe is a *work of creation*;
2) its course is under *Divine governance*; and
3) human beings are *images of God* (in the respect of having a *spiritual*, i.e., *non-material aspect*) to their nature.

Thus theists are restricted in what they can consistently believe about human origins and nature. While Pius XII and John Paul II were correct in saying that Christian doctrine is not in conflict with the general outlook of natural evolution, this, together with the latter's acceptance of evolution as a fact, risks creating a false sense of general compatibility; for belief in *creation, providence,* and *spiritual nature* is at odds with the developed positions advanced by many of the intellectual descendants of Darwin. Pius XII had distinguished between, on the one hand, "the doctrine of evolution, in as far as it inquires into the origin of the human body as coming from pre-existent and living matter" and on the other, a general evolutionary account of *all* aspects of human nature, and rejected the latter as incompatible with Christian teaching. Then John Paul II himself writes:

> theories of evolution which, because of the philosophies which inspire them, regard the spirit either as emerging from the forces of living matter, or as a simple epiphenomenon of that matter, are incompatible with the truth about man. They are therefore unable to serve as the basis for the dignity of the human person.[16]

16 "On Evolution," op. cit.

While species have evolved and the range of life-forms existing today and in the past is the result of variation and natural selection, it does not follow that the development of consciousness and the appearance of thinking, deliberating beings, are the product of purely physical processes leading to chance variations in replication. The latter reductionism not only goes beyond the empirical evidence but also includes claims about all processes being *physical*, and the course of biological evolution being due to *chance*, that could not be empirically confirmed since they are really philosophical theses presented under the guise of scientific ones. The issue of the historical emergence of mind is a philosophical one, in just the same way as is the issue of the relationship between mental and physical properties. Indeed, it is effectively the same issue seen in diachronic horizontal perspective rather than from a synchronic vertical standpoint.[17] Religious believers should not be intimidated by the assertion that "science has shown" that we are products of blind chance and entirely physical causes, and personalists should resist the idea that human minds differ from other parts of nature only in the complexity of their physical processes. But each should also set out to challenge the scientistic assumption wherever it is made, and expose its own difficulties. One such is that of accounting for the natural causal regularities that govern the operations of matter; another is that of explaining thought and moral action as involving nothing other than material processes.[18]

Wilhelm Dilthey observed that "we explain nature but we understand mental life."[19] In writing this he was reacting against the ambition of others, in particular Auguste Comte and John Stuart Mill, to develop a science of man that would formulate general

17 For more on this issue see "Mind over Matter" in ch. 2 of J. J. C. Smart and J. J. Haldane, *Atheism and Theism*, 2nd ed. (Oxford: Blackwell, 2003), 96–109.

18 Again see Smart and Haldane, *Atheism and Theism*, 111–115.

19 Wilhem Dilthey, "The Development of Hermeneutics," in *Dilthey: Selected Writings*, trans. and ed. H. P. Rickman (Cambridge: Cambridge University Press, 1976), 247–263.

laws of behavior and explain individual actions as instances of these causal regularities. His opposition to this form of "scientism" was influenced by Kant and Hegel, who likewise held that there is an important difference between the experimental, quantitative, and inductive methods of natural science and the meaning-discerning practices of the humanities. For Dilthey, it is of the nature of human beings to seek for meanings and purposes and to express these in their behavior, thus constituting the "life-world" (*Lebenswelt*). Accordingly, any study of distinctly human phenomena must be interpretative. By contrast, the domain of the natural sciences is one in which cause and quantity are all, and the comprehension of events is arrived at by discerning the structural properties of things and observing (or inferring) external relations between them. As the writer in the *Edinburgh Review* recognized, the difference and dignity of human persons lies not in a matter of degree or quantity but in a fundamental distinction of kind or quality, "a difference inscrutable from the point of view offered by [scientific naturalism], and only to be comprehended from the higher consideration."

VII. Towards a Philosophy of Higher Education

College and university education have been concerned with developing both scientific and humanistic understandings, and also an appreciation of the difference between these. Until relatively recently, such an education was the privilege of the few, but increasingly it is seen as a right of the many; and governments also favor mass participation in higher studies as contributing to economic and social development. This latter justification echoes one aspect of the Spencerian doctrine that I described at the outset, but it is also prey to the same criticism of instrumentalizing education. This contrasts with the views of others of the same period in English thought—including, as it happens, the most famous utilitarian: John Stuart Mill. If this seems surprising it is largely because the common representation of Mill as an amoral instrumentalist is unduly crude.

Two years before the publication of Darwin's *The Descent of Man*, the English writer Matthew Arnold published *Culture and Anarchy*. As well as being an important poet and social commentator, Arnold was also an inspector of schools and a professor at Oxford University. He saw *education*, in contrast to *technical training*, as being an essential means for the transmission of high culture, and he wrote of how being introduced to such culture is coming "to know the best that has been thought and said in the world" and he added the following:

> "[T]he idea which culture sets before us of perfection—
> an increased spiritual activity, having for its characters
> increased sweetness, increased light, increased life, in-
> creased sympathy—is an idea which the new democracy
> needs far more than the idea of the blessedness of the
> franchise, or the wonderfulness of their own industrial
> performances."[20]

This is a noble idea with which Augustine, Aquinas, and Newman—who also wrote on education in *de Magistro*, in *de Veritate*, and *The Idea of a University*—would certainly have agreed. It is also one, however, that can only be effectively pursued through the kind of intensive education and formation that involves a relatively small number of students in each class tutored by a widely read and committed teacher (not substitutable by online power point presentations and hand-outs). This combination is impossible in a mass higher education system; and the possibility of continuing to fund such a system even with lower educational ambitions is proving too much for the states of Western Europe.

Mill is best known, along with Jeremy Bentham, as one of the founders of utilitarianism and of modern liberalism; but two years before Arnold's publication of *Culture and Anarchy*, Mill delivered

---

20 Matthew Arnold, *Culture and Anarchy: An Essay in Political and Social Criticism* (1869) (Oxford: Oxford University Press, 2009), section I.

a long address on education at the University of St. Andrews in 1867 when he was elected Rector there by the student body. His speech lasted for three hours, which indicates much about Mill, about the students, and about the cultural standards of the time. What he said on that occasion connects with Arnold's concern with education as a civilizing and refining process. Mill thought that one of the main purposes of a university was to cultivate wisdom in those who were capable of it. This requires appropriate virtues on the part of both student and teacher, and a proper curriculum and syllabi structured around what Arnold had characterized as "the best that had been thought and said."

It is significant, I believe, that this understanding of the primary role of the university was most profoundly expressed in two texts which both originated in public lectures—that is lectures *to the public*, not just to academics; viz. Mill's Rectorial Address and John Henry Newman's *Idea of a University*, delivered as lectures in Dublin and first published in 1852 (with an extended edition in 1858), a decade and half earlier than Mill. From the perspective of the present, the most striking features of these two accounts of the nature and value of university education is what they *exclude*. Newman thought that it was not the business of universities to engage in research. He writes:

> [a university] is a place of teaching universal knowledge. This implies that its object is, on the one hand, intellectual, not moral; and, on the other, that it is the diffusion and extension of knowledge rather than the advancement of it. If its object were scientific and philosophical discovery, I do not see why a University should have students.[21]

Newman was not against research, but thought it should be conducted in special institutes. Mill likewise thought that the fact that

21 J. H. Newman, *Discourses on the Scope and Nature of a University* (Dublin: Duffy, 1852); *The Idea of a University* (New Haven, CT: Yale University Press, 1996), preface.

certain activities are important for individuals and society does not mean they should be part of the university curriculum. He writes that:

> [a university] is not a place of professional education. Universities are not intended to teach the knowledge required to fit men for some special mode of gaining their livelihood. Their object is not to make skillful lawyers, or physicians, or engineers, but capable and cultivated human beings. It is very right that there should be public facilities for the study of professions. But these things are no part of what every generation owes to the next, as that on which its civilisation and worth will principally depend.[22]

To understand these passages it is necessary to remind ourselves of the distinction between *knowledge* and *understanding*, and between the promotion and enhancement of welfare and the cultivation of the mind. Newman was concerned that, as well as coming to know about the *particular* and the *temporary*, human beings need to form an understanding of the *general* and the *permanent*. And to do that they need to develop powers of *abstraction* and *analogy* so as to reunite at an intellectual level what has become diversified at a scientific, technical, or practical one. This yields *understanding*, which is both an enduring constituent of human flourishing and an aid to various forms of practical life. Newman writes:

> When the intellect has once been properly trained and formed to have a connected view or grasp of things, it will display its powers with more or less effect according to its particular quality and capacity in the individual. In the case of most it makes itself felt in the good sense,

22 J.S. Mill, *Inaugural Address Delivered to the University of St. Andrews* (London: Longmans, Green, Reader and Dyer, 1867), 5.

sobriety of thought, reasonableness, candour, self-command and steadfastness of view which characterise it.[23]

The Newman/Mill/Arnold view, as indeed the Plato/Aristotle/Augustine/Aquinas idea (and I might add the Calvin/Knox idea) of education, has implications for the present day. First, we need to distinguish within higher education between the business of cultivating minds toward wisdom and that of conducting research, and again that of training people for specific forms of employment. Second, to specify more precisely and to implement that distinction in practice, one needs to confront the claim that university education is for the sake of economic benefit. This is something that academics are generally keen to dispute, institutional managers less so. But to reject the idea that universities are for the sake of economic prosperity is not to exclude such benefit as an anticipated or even desirable secondary effect. Next—and here academics are more likely to be divided—one needs to challenge the idea that good teaching is impossible unless teachers are also researchers. This notion is open to objection on several scores.

First, to keep abreast of one's subject requires scholarship, which is not the same as the pursuit and attainment of new knowledge, but may well take deeper learning and better judgment. Second, what is pursued under the heading of "research," at any rate in the arts, humanities, and social sciences, is often of dubious worth, being merely the accumulation of knowledge without proper regard to the goal of integrated understanding. Third, the mass of it does not much benefit fellow researchers, since the more that is produced the less (relatively) is consumed. The expansion in the number and size of universities over the last thirty years, along with the development of the "culture of research," has massively increased book and journal publication, and "research productivity" has been further increased by electronic publication. A recent survey estimated that over one million academic articles are published each year in some twenty-eight thousand journals (of which twenty thousand are peer

23 Newman, *Idea of a University*, preface.

reviewed). The average reported reading time for an article (and articles on average have grown longer) has decreased from forty-eight minutes per reading to thirty minutes.[24] Fourth, and in general terms, the more academics have the opportunity for research, the less they may wish to teach undergraduates, particularly undergraduates at the earliest stages of their studies, as contrasted with enlisting graduate students for their own expanding research projects.

To put the matter somewhat more boldly: the growing mass of researchers may have become a drag on, and even an obstacle to, the pursuit of the primary purpose of universities—namely, *education*. It impedes the effort to put students first and it consumes vast sums of private and public funding. How individuals and corporations choose to spend their resources is up to them, but how the state does is up to its citizens.

VIII. Educating for Wisdom

There is an interesting short story by the American author J. D. Salinger entitled *Franny*, in which the main character, after whom the story is named, is visiting an elite US university (Princeton) from her own smaller women's college (Smith, MA). Franny carries with her a copy of the Russian work *The Way of a Pilgrim* in which the narrator travels across Russia in search of spiritual fulfillment. Through Franny, we are invited to reflect upon the contrast between that search for wisdom, upon which she too is engaged, and the sapiential shallowness, or absence, she encounters at the heart of advanced higher education. She reflects as follows:

---

24 See M. Mabe and M. Amin, "Dr. Jekyll and Dr. Hyde: Author-Reader Asymmetries in Scholarly Publishing," *Aslib Proceedings* 54, no. 3 (2002): 149–157; C. Tenopir, D. King, S. Edwards and L. Wu, "Electronic Journals and Changes in Scholarly Article Seeking and Reading Patterns," *Aslib Proceedings: New Information Perspectives* 61, no. 1 (2009): 5–32; C. Tenopir, R. Mays and L. Wu, "Journal Article Growth and Reading Patterns," *New Review of Information Networking* 16, no. 1 (2011): 4–22.

I don't think it would have all got me quite so down if just once in a while—just once in a while—there was at least some polite little perfunctory implication that knowledge should lead to wisdom, and that if it doesn't, it's just a disgusting waste of time! But there never is! You never even hear any hints dropped on a campus that wisdom is supposed to be the goal of knowledge. You hardly ever even hear the word "wisdom" mentioned! ... In almost four years of college—and this is the absolute truth—in almost four years of college, the only time I can remember ever even hearing the expression "wise man" being used was in my freshman year, in Political Science! And do you know how it was used? It was used in reference to some nice old poopy elder statesman who'd made a fortune in the stock market and gone to Washington to be an adviser to President Roosevelt. Honestly, now! Four years of college, almost! I'm not saying that happens to everybody, but I just get so upset when I think about it I could die.[25]

It is particularly sobering to note that Salinger's story was first published in the *New Yorker Magazine* in 1955, which tells us that Franny's experience was not uncommon even then, and suggests one major source of the lead away from an understanding of universities as places for the cultivation of minds towards an idea of them as instruments of economic advantage or as places of research.

As the situation in the public finances worsens, hard choices will have to be made. It is hardly plausible to insist that education should continue to enjoy levels of support without obvious benefit to the undergraduates for whose sake the universities were brought into being, and who increasingly will have to pay for them. The theologians tell us that God does not will the evil, but permits it for the sake of the good that may come from it. Viewed in that perspective,

25 J. D. Salinger, *Franny and Zooey* (Boston: Little, Brown and Company, 1961).

the financial crises besetting Western countries due to personal and public debt, and the resulting fiscal contractions may yet bring forth benefits for the university if they cause us to engage in an overdue conversation about the value, aims, and purposes of education.[26]

Finally, if the university is to fulfill its role as a place for society to engage in reflection and self-criticism, then it needs to set aside the absurd posturing of those who would outdo one another in the extravagance of their claims. An example of this from the English-speaking world is the lecture by Richard Rorty entitled *An Ethics for Today*. Setting himself squarely against the Catholic Church and its tradition of moral objectivism rooted in a philosophical and theological anthropology, Rorty asks and answers a question. He writes:

> Is the Church right that there is such a thing as the structure of human existence, which can serve as a moral reference point? Or, do we human beings have no moral obligations except helping one another satisfy our desires, thus achieving the greatest possible amount of happiness . . . . There is nothing already in existence to which our moral ideals should try to correspond . . . . The answer to the question "are some human desires bad" is "no," but some desires do get in the way of our project of maximizing the overall satisfaction of desire . . . . *There is no such thing as an intrinsically evil desire.*[27] [my emphasis]

No intelligent and reflective person who is not a professional post-modernist academic really believes this, and many academics in the sciences think it as ridiculous as Rorty believed religion to

---

26 For some discussion of these matters set with a review of developments within educational studies since the early 1950s, see John Haldane, "Educational Studies and the Map of Philosophy," *British Journal of Educational Studies* 60, no. 1 (2012): 3–15.

27 Richard Rorty, *An Ethics for Today: Finding Common Ground Between Philosophy and Religion* (New York: Columbia University Press, 2010).

be. In consequence they take themselves to be justified in rejecting philosophy and theology alike, and not just these but the other humanities and arts subjects also, regarding them as, at best, forms of distracting entertainment. And so they are able to write as Stephen Hawking did in the passage from which I quoted earlier, and which I now repeat, but with a further sentence added:

> Philosophy [and natural theology] is dead. It has not kept up with modern developments in science, particularly physics, [and] scientists have become the bearers of the torch of discovery in our quest for knowledge . . . . Because there is a law of gravity, the Universe can and will create itself from nothing.[28]

The additional sentence serves to indicate why philosophy is needed if only to guard scientists from hubris and resulting nonsense, for what Hawking writes is as absurd in its own way as the nihilism of Rorty. Indeed, it is worse since it is literally incoherent. Nothing can create itself; *a fortiori,* nothing can create itself *ex nihilo!* In order to create, one first has to exist. The self-serving sensationalism of Rorty and Hawking both results from disconnecting academic research from the higher formation of the young on the one hand, and from respectful engagement with the non-academic, educated public on the other. Currently many academics and university managers are inclined to blame society for failing to support and respect them, but they have done much to lose the support of society and they now need to set about regaining it by showing how the university can be a site of formation and reflection: a place committed to *educating for wisdom.*[29]

28 Hawking and Mlodinow, *The Grand Design* (London: Bantam Press, 2010).

29 Portions of this essay appear in John Haldane, "Scientism and its Challenge to Humanism," *New Blackfriars* 93, no. 1048 (2012): 671–687.

Slow Wisdom as a Sub-Version of Reality
Walter Brueggemann

It was very late in the seventh century BCE for the ancient city of Jerusalem. It was very late, only a few years before the destruction of the city when its walls were breached, the temple destroyed, the king deported along with the royal family, and the political state of Judah ended.

It was very late for the ancient city of Jerusalem, because the city was being devoured by greedy corruption, of which the poet Jeremiah says,

> From the least to the greatest of them,
> everyone is greedy for unjust gain;
> and from prophet to priest,
> everyone deals falsely.
> They have treated the wound of my people carelessly,
> saying, "Peace, peace," when there is no peace.
> They acted shamefully, they committed abomination;
> yet they were not ashamed, they did not know how to
>   blush. (Jer. 6:13–15)

It was very late for the ancient city of Jerusalem, because the city was under threat at the hands of the aggressive Babylonian armies, of which the poet Jeremiah has God say:

> I am going to bring upon you a nation from far way,
> O house of Israel, says the Lord.
> It is an enduring nation,
> it is an ancient nation,
> a nation whose language you do not know,

nor can you understand what they say.
Their quiver is like an open tomb;
all of them are mighty warriors.
They shall eat up your harvest and your food;
they shall eat up your sons and your daughters;
they shall eat up your flocks and your herds;
they shall eat up your vines and your fig trees;
they shall destroy with the sword your fortified cities in
  which you trust. (Jer. 5:15–17)

This is only poetry. And the poet does not even name the coming enemy evoked by the will of God. The description of "a language you do not know" that will "eat up" all that you have sounds like al Qaeda; but it is likely, in context, Babylon.

More than merely condemning greedy corruption and external threat separately, the poetic tradition of Jeremiah dares to connect the two; *because* of greedy corruption, *therefore* the enemy threat; the God who presides over the historical process, in prophetic imagination, connects and enacts what we would analyze differently. The outcome of such odd reasoning is that *internal anti-neighborliness yields external risk and danger.*

I.

It is very late in Jerusalem, according to prophetic anticipation, and if one were such a poet as Jeremiah, what would one say after the poetry about greedy exploitation and after the poetry of external threat dispatched by holy resolve? Well, this is what the poet Jeremiah says in the midst of that lateness: "Do not let the wise boast in their wisdom, do not let the mighty boast in their might, do not let the wealthy boast in their wealth" (Jer. 9:23). The poet focuses on the great triad of control and pride, the three facets of having one's way in the world: might, wealth, and wisdom.

Might here means military force (*gibbor*), the capacity to control markets and natural resources. *Wealth* is the capacity to manage capital and impose requirements and restraints and leverage on all the others who live outside the constituency so that the whole of the global economy is ordered to flow toward us.

And then *wisdom*. We had not expected "wisdom" to come along with might and wealth, especially because our theme is wisdom and the work of the university is wisdom. Who can speak negatively of wisdom when we remember our great intellectual inheritance from the Greeks? But of course when wisdom is situated amid might and wealth, something decisive happens to wisdom. And of course that is what has happened among us. We have understood with Bacon that "knowledge is power" and we have transposed wisdom into knowledge that could control. That strange interplay of wisdom and knowledge brought the gift of the great scientific revolution in Bacon's time, and in its wake the great technological advances that have moved toward control that is never disinterested.

And before we knew it, Walter Isaacson and Evan Thomas had written a book entitled *The Wise Men*, a study of six of the titanic figures who have managed US foreign policy with Niebuhrian "critical realism" and have produced the abiding superpower—ample wisdom, ample might, and ample wealth—in order to be the chosen race in the modern world.[1] Perhaps inevitably, the great universities have signed on with that wisdom and have entered into compacts of wisdom that brought with them to the university the wealth of research grants and the power of connectedness.

And now we are sobered in this consultation, needing to take a deep breath concerning the way of Enlightenment wisdom/knowledge to which we have been pledged. That "wisdom" (as Isaacson and Thomas have called it) has led to immense power and wealth. But it has also led to the sad picture of Lyndon Johnson with his head in his hands, in his last days concerning Vietnam, completely exasperated about the ineffective power over which he presided. It has led to the verdict of the brothers McGeorge and William Bundy,

1   Walter Isaacson and Even Thomas, *The Wise Men: Six Friends and the World They Made* (New York: Simon and Schuster, 1986).

architects of the war, who wrote at the end of their book, "We were good, but we were not as good as we thought we were"; they may stand as an epitome of the hubris that has driven policy enwrapped in ideology. It led to the departure of the Wise Men from the White House after conferring with the president about Vietnam, and without a clue of what to do next. Then the oil spill, and the Japanese nuclear crisis, and the widespread suspicion that our technology has outrun our capacity to manage or even to think clearly; and now to us, who with deep anxiety seek scapegoats, along with zeal to dispose of "the other" among us—by violence, if necessary.

And the poet says:

> Do not boast about your might;
> Do not boast about your wisdom;
> Do not boast about your wealth.

II.

But what then? Well, if we take the antithesis of "might, wisdom, wealth," we might come up with a triad of "weakness, foolishness, and poverty." And of course that is what we get in Jesus of Nazareth:

> For God's foolishness is wiser than human wisdom, and God's weakness is stronger than human strength. (1 Cor. 1:25)

> For you know the generous act of our Lord Jesus Christ, that though he was rich, yet for your sakes he became poor, so that by his poverty you might become rich. (2 Cor. 8:9)

It turns out that the life of the Crucified One, in his body, exhibits the counterpoint to the great seduction of Jerusalem. He is the *embodiment of weakness* as he stood, vulnerable, before imperial authority. He is the *embodiment of foolishness*, as Terry Eagleton characterizes him:

Jesus, unlike most responsible American citizens, appears to do no work, and is accused of being a glutton and a drunkard. He is presented as homeless, propertyless, celibate, peripatetic, socially marginal, disdainful of kinsfolk, without a trade, a friend of outcasts and pariahs, averse to material possessions, without fear for his own safety, careless about purity regulations, critical of traditional authority, a thorn in the side of the establishment, and a scourge of the rich and powerful. . . . The morality Jesus preaches is reckless, extravagant, improvident, over-the-top, a scandal to actuaries and a stumbling block to real estate agents; forgive your enemies, give away your cloak as well as your coat, turn the other cheek, love those who insult you, walk the extra mile, take no thought for tomorrow.[2]

He is the *embodiment of poverty*, nowhere to lay his head, no property or even health care.

The remembered Jesus sits amid our posturing and reminds us that the great imperial triad of might, wisdom, and wealth, a triad celebrated in ancient Israel since Solomon, never delivers the security or the happiness that it promises.

III.

But I will not linger over that counter-triad of *weakness, foolishness, and poverty* that waits silently for us, because that triad is too outrageous and too remote for the business at hand. Instead, I will consider the counter-triad that Jeremiah, in his poetry, lines out. His triad is fully congruent with that of Jesus, but it has a kind of available realism that is lacking in Jesus of Nazareth, a realism that permits people like us at least to take it seriously: "But let those who boast in this, that they understand and know me, that I am

2 Terry Eagleton, *Reason, Faith, and Revolution: Reflections on the God Debate* (New Haven: Yale University Press, 2009), 10; 14.

the Lord; I act with steadfast love, justice, and righteousness in the earth, for in these things I delight, says the Lord" (Jer. 9:24). This counter-triad is rooted in the reality of the Lord, the God of Israel, who is celebrated as the great deliverer from slavery and the creator of heaven and earth. And, says the poet, even in the midst of greedy corruption and external threat, some know. They are the ones who boast of my stuff; they know me. They have entered into covenant with me. They have acknowledged my will and my purpose, and they understand me; they can factor out the implications of who I am and what I will. That is what makes the tradition endlessly compelling. They are the ones who give Jerusalem trouble through the night and buoyancy through the day. What they know and understand, says the poet, is that I act with *steadfast love, justice, and righteousness;* I delight in those things. And because I delight in them and am pleased when they appear, this people and this city are under mandate to live them out. Out of the deep covenantal tradition of Israel the poet offers a *triad of fidelity* that stands counter to the *triad of control* that was destroying Israel.

It is very late in Jerusalem, but nobody knows if it is too late. Sometimes the poets, including Jeremiah, said it was too late—too late for the Ethiopians to change their skin, too late for the leopard to change its spots, too late for the Solomonic regime to repent of its might, wisdom, and wealth, too late because of the internal corruption and the external threat (Jer. 13:23). At other times, however, these same poets, including Jeremiah, knew that it was late but not too late. The urgent task was to move the body politic, with its marching armies, and its blessing priests, and its cunning scribes, away from the triad of control toward the triad of covenantal fidelity. And, when that move is made, then a new historical possibility might yet be available; but it is very late.

The university sits in a society where it is very late, in a society that is largely committed to the triad of *might, wisdom, and wealth;* and, in some measure, the university, like the church, has colluded with that triad to its great benefit. The lateness of hour, I suggest, invites the university, like the wayward son in a far country, to come to its senses, to remember its home and its belonging and its vocation, to live alertly and knowingly in a very late moment amid these competing triads of control and fidelity, knowing that both are powerful and compelling and that both are indispensable. But because the triad of control has carried the day in our society without much critical reflection, it may be the great tilt of the university to give privilege and priority to the triad of fidelity that has nearly disappeared from the public face of our society, as it had disappeared from the ancient city of Jerusalem. It will be my purpose here to lay out in as many ways as I can, *the interface of these two triads* that concerned the poet and that might usefully concern us in a society where it is very late.

When we think about wisdom, we engage two competing notions: the wisdom of Enlightenment control on the one hand, and that other ancient wisdom rooted in "the fear of the Lord," two wisdoms that will yield two very different worlds. The wisdom of control we may call *fast wisdom*; it assumes that we are free to manage and shape and administer and master the world according to our own interest. The wisdom of fidelity I will call *slow wisdom*; it is wisdom that waits and watches and receives and yields and hopes.[3] Fast wisdom, now paced by electronic urgency, concerns knowing and having and possessing and controlling. Slow wisdom is about serious, engaged relatedness that simply will not be

3 On "slowness," see Walter Mosley, "Ten Things You Should Know about Slow," *The Nation* (December 13, 2010), 8. He lists the following:

> 1. Say no to fast food and join the Slow Food movement instead.
> 2. Slow down to the speed limit when driving.
> 3. Slow down your conversation.
> 4. Be slow to judge.
> 5. Tune in, not out.
> 6. Not so fast—do you really need a new [fill in the blank]?
> 7. Wouldn't you rather meditate than medicate?
> 8. Take the time to read poetry daily.
> 9. Take time to consider the children.
> 10. Don't rush through life.

hurried. It matters decisively whether the world is "figured" by fast-paced control that breeds greed and resentment, or by slow-paced wisdom that hosts complexity and refuses sound bites. The task of the university, I suggest, is to mediate and adjudicate between these triads and to expose the risks and hazards of the triad of control that has brought our society to the brink of default that is not only financial but also moral. The ancient city was in a moral default that could not be sustained. It is no wonder that the old poets, given how late it was, wondered if it was too late, or only very late.

IV.

Here then, in eight phrasings, is my exposition of the impact and future-generating potential of these two triads: *the triad of control: might, wisdom, and wealth; and the triad of fidelity: steadfast love, justice, and righteousness.* In each case I will, as you would expect, tilt toward the latter. Pursuing the triad of fidelity is, in my judgment, the urgent challenge we face in our belated time.

First, the triad of fidelity focuses on the body, whereas the triad of control focuses, characteristically, on abstractions of power and possession. The couplet of "justice and righteousness" (two members of the former triad) are concerned with the ways in which the resources of the community are mobilized for the bodily reality of persons and the healthy reality of the body politic. The materiality of the biblical tradition has to do with the quotidian dimension of the vulnerable: the widow, the orphan, the immigrant, and the poor, and the wherewithal to sustain a common life of dignity and well-being.[4] Thus the indictment of the ancient city:

> They have grown fat and sleek.
> They know no limits in deeds of wickedness;

---

4   Nicholas Wolterstorff, *Justice: Rights and Wrongs* (Princeton: Princeton University Press, 2008), 75–82, terms these four groups "the quartette of the vulnerable."

they do not judge with justice
the cause of the orphan, to make it prosper,
and they do not defend the right of the needy. (Jer. 5:28)

And thus, the same poet's summons to possibility:

If you truly amend your ways and your doings, if you
truly act justly one with another, if you do not oppress
the alien, the orphan, and the widow, or shed innocent
blood in this place, and if you do not go after other gods
to your own hurt, then . . . (Jer. 7:5–7)

Justice concerns seeing to the bodily needs of the vulnerable by
ordering the body politic differently. "Righteousness" is weigh-
ing in for the well-being of the community. The poetic tradition
always cares about food, clothing, and housing. The materiality
of the ancient poets' triad refuses the requirements of "ideas,
concepts, theories, and ideologies" that draw energy away from
the reality of those who stand in front of us. The flight to abstraction is an endless seduction of those in control, so that social reality can be reduced to a program or a budget that
depends always upon euphemism to hide the bodily reality of
those next door. The seduction of the university, not unlike the
government and the church, is to traffic in abstraction, and the
challenge of the university is to bring energy back to that quotidian reality so that resources and passion may be mobilized
differently.

Second, the triad of fidelity focuses on the neighborhood,
whereas the triad of control is drawn to the club. The "club" is a
staging ground and device for exclusion, so that one need deal only
with those one chooses, with those most like us. It is a mark of
privilege that brings with it the sense of knowing best and being
right. It proceeds by exclusion to screen out the other—variously
women, or blacks, and surely the poor. Of course the universities,
the "best ones," have been no more hospitable than clubs with their
exclusionary quotas.

But the neighborhood takes in all of us who move up and down the street. There is an egalitarian assumption about the legitimacy of all its members present, and the sharing of resources to which all are entitled. Historically, of course, without romanticizing, a rural community—before social stratification, acute division of labor, and the development of surplus value—was a more or less egalitarian community (with the notable exception of the doctor who lived in the big house). But the urban reality of social stratification, acute division of labor, and the accumulation of surplus wealth has largely destroyed that sense of neighborly egalitarianism.

And of course the university is deeply enmeshed in that crisis. For admission is a ticket to entitlement. Because we can no longer have affirmative action, as the urban elite court has ruled, the privileged who come from better schools are better prepared for application; therefore, on the basis of socially constructed "merit," only they occupy the space and the fellowships. We produce a class of "managers of social symbols" (of which I am a member), with only a vague memory of real "work." The process of privilege and entitlement evokes a stream of influence that eventually culminates in might and wealth based on a certain kind of wisdom. And of course such a trajectory of control will hide behind a hundred defenses of pedigree, certification, gated communities, tenure, and all the rest.

But the cadences of steadfast love concern "the neighbors" who are bound together in common need, common resources, and common destiny, pledged to common goods that will not give credence to these enduring distinctions. I am most taken with the arguments and attestations of my new colleagues Peter Block and John McKnight, who focus on the mobilization of the neighborhood, by which they mean quite concretely the folk on the block.[5] Their mode of "asset based community" is committed to the proposition

5   John McKnight and Peter Block, *The Abundant Community: Awakening the Power of Families and Neighborhoods* (San Francisco: Berrett-Koehler Publishers, 2010).

that the neighborhood, rightly mobilized, has all the assets necessary for the sustenance of a healthy existence. Their repeated insistence is that it is more adequate to rely on the wisdom of a neighbor
than it is to rely on the wisdom of an expert, so that again we come
face to face with competing modes of wisdom.

Of course I am aware that every college and university has endless program opportunities through which students can participate
in and experience the neighborhood on the ground. But we all
know, as students know, that such opportunities are marginal and
incidental, and at best extraneous to the real pay-outs of education.

But we have, in very recent time, witnessed the failure of the
club. We have witnessed it in bailouts in which ordinary taxpayers
footed the bill for the privileged, who go right on with their excessive privilege. And it will not do! Thus, I suspect that a shift of emphasis from one triad to the other is a deep and systemic work in
the university. In the emergent awareness that the might, wisdom,
and wealth of the club has in fact failed, we fall back on the wisdom of the neighborhood that finds might in vulnerability and
health in generosity—vulnerability and generosity that are remote
from the culture of the club that is prone to deny vulnerability and
is organized against generosity.

Third, the triad of fidelity is deeply situated in the tradition,
whereas the triad of control traffics in the reasoning of syllogism
and memo. Syllogisms reflect controlling reasoning that yields a
kind of thin certitude about which there is no argument and nothing of steadfast love. Memos are unambiguous notes of power; wit-
ness David's memo to Joab that was a death sentence for Uriah (2
Sam. 11:14–15) and Jezebel's memo that was a death sentence for
Naboth (1 Kgs. 21:8–10). Such writing as control is knowingly reflected in Steinbeck's *Grapes of Wrath* when the Okies observe that,
whenever the man with the clipboard writes something down, they
own less. Of course that process of writing memos continues in our
time—notices from the bank, etc. etc.—all of whose writers would
like to be neighborly, but the rules preclude it.

Since the seventeenth century, such reasoning has declared war
on tradition.[6] And now that assault on tradition continues in the

reduction of reality to sound bites, the praise of the church to "praise hymns," and the delete button that can erase into innocent amnesia. But communities of steadfast love, justice, and righteousness, by contrast, have long memories and deep hopes, and do not believe that instantaneous satisfaction is an adequate displacement for remembering and anticipating.

In Jeremiah, the tradition is called "the way":

> Let me go to the rich
> And speak to them;
> Surely they know the way of the Lord,
> the law of their God. (Jer. 5:5)

> And then, if they will diligently learn the ways of my people, to swear by my name, "As the Lord lives" . . . then they shall be built up in the midst of my people. (Jer. 12:16)

> See, I am setting before you the way of life and the way of death. (Jer. 21:8)

The last text is a deliberate echo of Deut. 30:15–10—the way of life and death, the way of blessing and curse. Broadly construed, the way refers to the Torah of the Lord, not only commandments, but instruction and lore. The way is voiced at the beginning of the Psalter:

> Happy are those who do not follow the advice of the
> wicked,
> or take the path that sinners tread,
> or sit in the seat of scoffers;
> but their delight is in the law [Torah] of the Lord,
> and on his law [Torah] they meditate day and night.
> (Ps. 1:1–2)

6   See Paul Hazard, *The European Mind: The Critical Years 1680–1715* (New York: Fordham University Press, 1990).

The "way" (Torah) is the entire legacy of being bound in covenantal fidelity and covenantal obedience to the Creator who has ordered the world so that it will not be mocked. This order provides that personal practice and public policy in the life of Israel will cohere with the transcendent purposes of God.

The force of Torah aims to resist autonomy, wherein one imagines unfettered freedom without responsibility or restraint—freedom to seize what belongs to another and to exploit the neighbor who may be vulnerable. In the end, the Torah is Israel's testimony to the covenantal shape of created existence. The world is organized according to steadfast love. The economy is to be engaged according to neighborly justice which begins with "You shall not covet" (Exod. 20:17). The political culture is to be shaped by righteousness that is the work of the common good. The entire purpose of liberal arts is to help the students situate themselves in tradition that refuses the autonomy of Enlightenment reason with its concomitant of consumer seduction.

The triad of fidelity eschews the seduction of the reasoning of autonomy; it also fends off the counter-temptation of absolutism that is so powerful in our society. It refuses absolutism through the ongoing disputatious practice of interpretation. Thus the book of Deuteronomy, the great background in the tradition of the poet Jeremiah, is essentially a model and early practice of hermeneutics: "Not with our ancestors did the Lord make this covenant, but with us, who are all of us here alive today" (Deut. 5:3). The old Torah cannot just be read. Nor can there be recourse, as we are now wont to take, to "original intention"—for such so-called "originalism" is a complete misconstrual of the nature of tradition. Thus it is the great work of the university to nurture responsible, wise, competent hermeneutists who refuse the easy relativism of popular culture and who refuse, with equal resolve, the temptation to absolutism, whether that of God or country or sect or system. The tradition requires interpretive agility that knows that the memory is a beginning point, but never a conclusion; an interpretive assumption made clear by the rabbi who taught, "You have heard it said of old, but I say unto you." Rightly understood, the tradition is always being reformulated in radical contemporaneity, but with deep roots that are honored, and not deleted, by interpretation. The ancient paths, the paths trod in the neighborhood, often over-ridden in the club, give thickness to the human process, a thickness without which we cannot live for very long.

Fourth, the triad of fidelity attends to pain whereas the triad of control specializes in numbness. The interface of pain and numbness is poignantly voiced in the sobbing of failed Jerusalem:

> Is it nothing to you, all you who pass by?
> Look and see
> if there is any sorrow like my sorrow, which was brought
>   upon me,
> which the Lord inflicted on the day of his fierce anger.
>   (Lam. 1:12)

The city voices its loss and grief, but then notices that passersby, the other nations, do not acknowledge. Is it nothing to you? The triad of control, like the priest or the Levite on the way to Jericho, in its numbness, does not notice. It passes by on the other side. It has faster errands to run. It has reduced pain to a statistic, suffering to the cost of doing business. The practice of abusive power, ex-ploitative economics, devastating militarism, and the disturbance of the vulnerable earth must continue, even if the pain therein pro-duced requires denial, all in the interest of might and wealth. The denial is based on the race to domination, and we cannot afford to linger very long in the hurt.

When such denial is pushed far enough, it becomes numbness, the frozenness of the human capacity to stand in solidarity. Robert Lifton is our master teacher of what he has termed "psychic numb-ing," the shutdown of emotional depth in order to survive; circum-stance requires that we "quit feeling."[7] Lifton has studied, variously, Hiroshima, Auschwitz, Viet Nam veterans, and the anx-iety over nuclear threat during the Cold War. He devised the phrase

---

7   For a narrative summary of Lifton's work, see Robert Jay Lifton, *Wit-ness to an Extreme Century: A Memoir* (New York: Free Press, 2011).

"psychic numbing" to describe the strategy of staying sane in a world of insane violence.

The alternative to such numbing is to hear and touch and honor the pain that arises from what Lifton calls "atrocity-producing" policies, systems, and attitudes. It is pain that lives beneath the surface of the world of might, wisdom, and wealth. The triad of fidelity, perhaps, begins in that moment at the start of the Exodus narrative. The slaves eventually cry out. They cry out because they suffer abuse at the hands of Pharaoh, a vigorous practitioner of might, wisdom, and wealth. They cry out; and then comes this holy response:

> God heard their groaning, and God remembered his covenant with Abraham, Isaac, and Jacob. God looked upon the Israelites, and God took notice of them. (Exod. 2:24–25)

The wonder of this triad is that God hears, God notices, God remembers, God witnesses. God acts in solidarity. The story of faith is the story of divine solidarity with human suffering, an alliance against the drama of control. In that instant of holy notice, the steadfast love of God is evoked. God bends God's self toward the suffering of Israel and, derivatively, toward the suffering of the world. And then God acts in justice and righteousness to sustain steadfast love, an act that challenges systemic covetousness and that terminates the totalizing regime of Pharaoh, who is the biblical model for numbness.

But of course this triad of fidelity does not remain at a religious level. We can trace the cry and the holy response as it traverses the world of might and wealth. Just after the Ten Commandments, Moses warns Israel about psychic numbness that receives an economic articulation:

> You shall not wrong or oppress a resident alien, for you were aliens in the land of Egypt. You shall not abuse any widow or orphan. If you do abuse them, when they cry

out to me, I will surely heed their cry; my wrath will burn, and I will kill you with the sword, and your wives shall become widows and your children orphans. If you lend money to my people, to the poor among you, you shall not deal with them as a creditor; you shall not exact interest from them. If you take your neighbor's cloak in pawn, you shall restore it before the sun goes down; for it may be your neighbor's only clothing to use as cover; in what else shall that person sleep? And if your neighbor cries out to me, I will listen, for I am compassionate. (Exod. 22:21–27)

These two laws focus on the vulnerable, who are always our primary candidates for pain. The first law is a generic protection of immigrants, widows, and orphans. The second is a specific warning about extorting the poor with excessive interest on loans. Both laws anticipate that the vulnerable, when abused, will cry out. They will cry out, and the totalizing system of numbness and denial cannot silence them. In the first, it is anticipated that God will hear the cry of the abused and retaliate. In the second, it is anticipated that God will hear and have compassion. Either way, it is the attentiveness of God that will subvert the ordered world of numbness. The future is open to the God who is not numbed.

The university runs the risk of alliance with the interests of might, wisdom, and wealth, a practice of knowledge "from above" that treats the cry as a necessary inconvenience. It is possible, however, that the university may be a venue in which the long history of the subversive cry of pain is hosted, so that the long literature of truth and hurt is received and honored as a contemporary script. Preoccupation with the cry is natural in the humanities; but it is no less urgent in the social sciences, in economics, and in the earth sciences where the earth itself cries out about the abuse. Given this interface, the question that might haunt the university as it might haunt us all is this: "Is it nothing to you, all you who pass by?" The prophet Amos provides an inventory of the kinds of self-preoccupations that narcotize and keep us busy not noticing:

> Alas for those who lie on beds of ivory,
> and lounge on their couches,
> and eat lambs from the flock,
> and calves from the stall;
> who sing idle songs to the sound of the harp,
> and like David improvise on instruments of music;
> and drink wine from bowls,
> and anoint themselves with the finest oils . . . (Amos 6:4–6a)

Amos offers a sketch of affluent self-indulgence. But the accent falls on the indictment that follows: " . . . but are not grieved over the ruin of Joseph." That is, they do not notice that society is practicing an order of death, and so going to hell in a hand basket. And then the poetry voices the big, inexplicable leap in anticipation: "Therefore they shall now be the first to go into exile" (v. 7). Those who do not notice will be the ones displaced, because the cry pulses in the historical process and the numbing finally will not prevail.

Fifth, the triad of fidelity specializes in dreams that are not held back by circumstance, whereas the triad of control takes life as a present possession to be guarded and kept to perpetuity by the entitled few. The totalizing system of those who make the rules, manage the money, administer the power, and mobilize their wisdom is evident everywhere among us. That totalizing system aims to maintain and enhance advantage over others. The capacity to control and own to perpetuity through deregulation, and through stacking of the cards by law and ruthless predatory management, finally ends in a society that is short of social possibility. Thus it is that Pharaoh, in his totalizing sovereignty, can finally assert in an illusionary fashion: "My Nile is my own; I made it for myself" (Ezek. 29:3). He forgets that the Nile, like every proximate source of life, is a gift that can never be possessed.

So it is with Jezebel who says to her pouting husband-king: "Do you now govern Israel? Get up, eat some food, and be cheerful; I will give you the vineyard of Naboth the Jezreelite" (1 Kgs. 21:7). Are you not king? Are you not entitled? Do you not possess the leverage to have what you want? She imagines that the land is her gift to give to Ahab. And when she has done her nefarious manipulation, she says to her wimpish husband: "Go, *take possession* of the vineyard of Naboth the Jezreelite, which he refused to give you for money; for Naboth is not alive, but dead" (v. 15; emphasis added). And the narrator adds: "As soon as Ahab heard that Naboth was dead, Ahab set out to go down to the vineyard of Naboth the Jezreelite, to *take possession* of it" (v. 16; emphasis added). It is all about possession, what we may call "realized eschatology": the belief that what we have is permanent, to be secured through seizure and then protected through entitlement.

And from beneath the world of possessions comes the cadence of dream. Dream is always inherently subversive of present arrangement. The dream already intruded into the sleep of the ancient pharaoh who had everything. And then he dreamed seven lean, sickly cows and seven blighted shocks of wheat, which together signified seven lean years of famine to come (Gen. 41:1–32). No less Nebuchadnezzar, who had it all; it was during the night, by the dream of a tree that was cut down, that he was driven by his power to insanity (Dan. 4:19–33). The dream was enough to destabilize the most stable of regimes.

The prophets, who do not "predict," are the voices of God's dream. They say with some frequency, "In that day . . . " or "The days are surely coming . . . . " The day to come is a day of disarmament when they shall beat their swords into plowshares and their spears into pruning hooks (Isa. 2:4); they will not learn war anymore. The days are coming when the Lord will act against all hubris:

> For the Lord of hosts has a day
> against all that is proud and lofty,
> against all that is lifted up and high;
> against all the cedars of Lebanon, lofty and lifted up;
> and against all the oaks of Bashan;
> against all the high mountains, and
> against all the lofty hills;

against every high tower,
and against every fortified wall. (Isa. 2:12–15)

The days are coming, say the dreamers, and they cannot be stopped. They are powered by a holy resolve that stands outside our possession in a way that is incessantly subversive. If we trace the dream of subversion far enough, we can follow it to Martin Luther King, Jr. at the Lincoln monument. He said repeatedly, "I have a dream . . . . " The reason we remember the cadences of his dream speech is that we know his is the dream of our society writ deep; it is the dream of God for justice and righteousness and steadfast love. Like all such dreamers, Martin had no clue how to get from here to there. He only knew that the dream had substance and force and authority, and could not be stopped. This trajectory of poets imagines that the dream is still under way, still overcoming apartheid, still working for the dignity of the weak, still demanding equity for the poor, still ensuring an end to the systemic violence that we call policy.

The university is always deciding how much it will serve the forces of possession. It must do so, but it also must do other than that and more than that, because the world is not closed into present arrangements. The world does not stand still simply because we arrive at our preferred arrangement. Francis Fukuyama opined that, with the fall of the Soviet Union, history had come to an end, and that the force of liberal democratic capitalism had ultimately prevailed.[8] But of course, the dreamers know that the world does not end that way. It ends, rather, when the full drama is actualized among us:

Go and tell John what you have seen and heard: the blind receive their sight, the lame walk, the lepers are cleansed, the deaf hear, the dead are raised, the poor have good news brought to them. (Luke 7:22)

8   Francis Fukuyama, *The End of History and the Last Man* (New York: Free Press, 1992).

The world is always breaking open beyond possession to dream. The dream is always violating our arrangements of power, to discover new power from below. The dream is always breaking our wisdom with new awarenesses that arise among the lowly, who generate the most poignant poetry. And we, in our entitlements, are always juggling our possessions, because the dream has a bite, even for us.

Sixth, the triad of fidelity majors in imagination while the triad of control specializes in explanation. Of course we must do both imagination and explanation. We have known that since the great German hermeneutists, Humboldt and Dilthey. But in a world of technological reductionism and positive reason, explanation comes to contain everything. In a world of explanation, education consists of mastering the rules and procedures for linear clarity in order to get ahead in the current system. Explanation, essential as it is, in the end is a strategy for accumulation of what the system offers. And then the effort is to make it more so—more might, more wealth, more wisdom of the same kind—and life becomes an anxious pursuit of such treasure.

Imagination, by contrast, is the capacity to host and voice a world other than the one that is in front of us. In my discipline of Old Testament studies, historical criticism—important as it has been—has been a long-term German enterprise of management, containment, and accommodation, making the text fit the reason of this age. Happily, in a post-critical move, we now have ventures in Scripture study that do not force the text into an explanatory straitjacket, but can hear that the text, in some great measure, is an act of subversive imagination, hosting and bringing to voice another world, other than the one that is in front of us.[9] That is why preaching is so politically dangerous, and why regimes must keep a lid on Scripture. And that is why, in the end, the triad of control in our modern world has preferred historical critical approaches that keep the dangerous force of such imagination in the remote past.

---

9   See Walter Brueggemann, "Where Is the Scribe?," *The Anglican Theological Review* 93, no. 3 (Summer 2011): 385–403.

But it turns out—as Michael Walzer, the great Jewish political philosopher, has seen—that the Exodus narrative is not a report on an ancient emancipation.[10] It is, rather, a narrative anticipation of many liberations that are yet to be acted. It turns out that Pharaoh is neither Rameses II nor Merneptah; Pharaoh is whoever sits atop the pyramid of might, wisdom, and wealth to the disadvantage of the laborers who are treated ruthlessly. It turns out that the Exodus event was a divine stirring in South Africa, where there was no chance against the apartheid regime, and the leadership for steadfast love had Egyptian names like Nelson and Desmond. The script of steadfast love, justice, and righteousness that eventuates in freedom, dignity, and equity is a script that continues to be performed in bodily dramas of courage and hope.

It turns out that the manna story is not simply a report on an ancient heaven-sent miracle, though it is that. It is also—in postcolonial reading—an act of recognition that all the bread needed— Bread for the World—is not the property of the cartel that stores the grain and owns the bakery. It turns out that the only Bread for the World that will meet the hunger of humanity is broken bread, bread that has shattered the citadels of might and wealth, bread that by its abundance and its generosity refuses imperial production and elitist distribution.

Explanatory education reads backward to tell us how it was and how it will be, world without end. Imaginative education reads forward toward unthought possibilities—not fantasy, not escapism, not denial of what is, but the complex, irrefutable surging of newness that is inherent in God's ordering of creation. It will not do much good to debate evolution. But it will do much good to notice the pulsing of new possibilities of steadfast love, justice, and righteousness that all the dogs and the surveillance and the weapons cannot stop.

Michael Walzer has written in his book on the Exodus narrative: first, that wherever you live, it is probably Egypt; second, that

10 Michael Walzer, *Exodus and Revolution* (New York: Basic Books, 1985).

there is a better place, a world more attractive, a promised land; and third, that "the way to the land is through the wilderness." There is no way to get from here to there except by joining together and marching.[11] Walzer has offered an interpretive possibility that has been enacted many times in our own lifetime among those not enthralled by might, wisdom, and wealth. Our contemporary "marching" has run from the Freedom Rides to the Velvet Revolution to Yeltsin atop the tank, and the March from Selma to the hope-filled in Cairo and among the victims of apartheid who keep singing, and now with the 99% on Wall Street:

> We are marching in the light of God,
> We are marching in the light of God.
> We are marching in the light of God.
> We are marching, we are marching in the light of God.[12]

But the narrative of emancipation is performed not only in the streets. It is performed wherever the rule of law tames the predators; it is evident in the Helsinki Declaration of Human Rights; it is enacted in government and private sector initiatives that break patterns of exploitation. What kind of a "school of imagination" is it that has produced such marchers, such advocates as the people in the book of Acts who keep appearing before imperial authority to testify to the surge of new life that they have glimpsed in Easter? What kind of education nurtures so that explanation does not default on the possibilities of newness that have been entrusted to us? We have narrative models; but we have no blueprints, because blueprints run almost immediately to explanation.

Seventh, the triad of fidelity invites to a vocation whereas the triad of control envisions a career. The trajectory of might, wisdom, and wealth is all about joining the firm, fitting in, and advancing. It is about the good fortune of having someone at the club or in the admissions office saying, "You will want to look out for this

---

11 Ibid., 149.
12 "We Are Marching in the Light of God," *The New Century Hymnal* (Cleveland: Pilgrim Press, 1995), 526.

young lady." Such connectedness of course is not bad, and we all would wish for it. But it is, almost invariably, an invitation to go along and get along. By contrast, a vocation, when it is authentic, is a summons outside the box from someone with deep authority, who calls and summons and propels beyond one's own intention to larger purpose. And of course human history is made by those called, all the way back to Moses who was addressed from the bush.

The pressure in higher education now is all about career and practical study in order to make a good living. The university, moreover, must justify itself in terms of earning power. But of course, the university at its best is not just about making a living, but about making a life that is deeper and more serious than the next advancement in might and wealth.

The best case study I know for this interface of career and calling is the young Daniel, a Jew who lived amid Babylonian (or Persian or Hellenistic) might, wisdom, and power. He was recruited into the civil service of the empire by Nebuchadnezzar and he advanced rapidly to great influence. It is astonishing how many of his narrative episodes end with yet another imperial promotion:

> In every matter of wisdom and understanding concerning which the king inquired of them, he found them ten times better than all the magicians and enchanters in his whole kingdom. And Daniel continued there until the first year of King Cyrus. (Dan. 1:20–21)

> Then the king promoted Daniel, gave him many great gifts, and made him ruler over the whole province of Babylon and chief prefect over all the wise men of Babylon . . . Daniel remained at the king's court. (2:48–49)

> Then the king promoted Shadrach, Meshach, and Abednego in the province of Babylon. (3:30) Then Belshazzar gave the command, and Daniel was clothed in purple, a chain of gold was put around his neck, and a proclamation

was made concerning him that he should rank third in the kingdom. (5:29)

So this Daniel prospered during the reign of Darius and the reign of Cyrus the Persian. (6:28)

What a career! He made it big in the empire, under Nebuchadnezzar and Belshazzar, the Babylonians; and under Darius and Cyrus, the Persians. What is clear, at the same time, is that Daniel's calling to be a faithful Jew in the service of the God of Heaven remained uncompromised. In chapter 1, Daniel refused imperial food so that he would not be "defiled" (1:8). In chapter 2, even the king worships Daniel's God to whom Daniel had prayed for wisdom:

The king said to Daniel, "Truly, your God is God of gods and Lord of kings and a revealer of mysteries, for you have been able to reveal this mystery!" (2:47)

In chapter 3, the three friends of Daniel act defiantly against the empire for the sake of their God:

O Nebuchadnezzar, we have no need to present a defense to you in this matter. If our God whom we serve is able to deliver us from the furnace of blazing fire and out of your hand, O King, let him deliver us. But if not, be it known to you, O king, that we will not serve your god and we will not worship the golden statue that you have set up. (3:16–18)

In chapter 4, Nebuchadnezzar worships the God of Daniel:

Now I, Nebuchadnezzar, praise and extol and honor the
    King of heaven,
  for all his works are truth,
  and his ways are justice;

and he is able to bring low
those who walk in pride. (4:37)

In chapter 6, Darius worships the God of Daniel:

I make a decree, that in all my royal dominion people
should tremble and fear before the God of Daniel. (6:26)

No doubt the intention of the Daniel narrative is to make the
case that one can be a good faithful Jew and still prosper in the empire. *Mutatis mutandis*, one can live amid the regime of might, wisdom, and wealth but still be a practitioner of steadfast love, justice,
and righteousness.

In the case of Daniel's three friends, the narrative subtly reminds us of the maintenance of an identity and a vocation that do
not give into the empire. We know the three friends as Meshach,
Shadrach, and Abednego. But those names that are familiar to us
are names assigned to these Jews by the empire:

The palace master gave them other names: Daniel he
called Belteshazzar, Hananiah he called Shadrach,
Mishael he called Meshach, and Azariah he called Abednego. (1:7)

But those are not their real, Jewish names. The preceding verse at-
tests their real Jewish names:

Among them were Daniel, Hananiah, Mishael, and
Azariah, from the tribe of Judah. (1:6)

And those Jewish names are repeated in Dan. 2:17 as the narrator
still remembers.

Thus, the struggle for identity. Perhaps we might judge that
these four handsome young Jews maintained a double identity and
lived a double life: imperial by day and Jewish by night, imperial
in the market, Jewish in the synagogue. Or perhaps they gave in

and forgot their Jewish names and identities. Or perhaps they pretended with their career names but knew their true vocational names. Either way, the matter is complex, now as then. Either way, education may help people struggle with an identity and a vocation. In our context, it is either the name imposed by consumer ideology or the preservation of baptismal name assigned to make us, as we say in my church, "Sealed as Christ's own forever." Education is about name and identity, true identity and imposed identity. Clearly the names to which we answer are determined by the triad in which we are situated, a faith identity amid steadfast love, justice, and righteousness; an empire-given identity amid might, wisdom, and wealth. The issue of identity is complex; it is clear, nonetheless, that education that aims only at serving the totalizing regime of wealth and might will never yield a covenantal identity that can respond to the divine impetus for mercy and compassion and generosity.

And finally, it is written in Ps. 19:10 concerning the truth and power of God's commandments:

> More to be desired are they than gold,
> even much fine gold;
> sweeter also than honey,
> and drippings of the honeycomb. (v. 10)

We may take this statement as an epitome of the pair of triads I have exposited. The psalm speaks in many synonyms of Torah (decrees, precepts, commandments, fear of the Lord, ordinances), many ways to signify the transcendent purpose of God that orders life toward well-being. This offer is "better," more to be desired; it is better than gold, even much fine gold. It is better than honey, the drippings from a honeycomb. Imagine, thick guidance to covenantal existence, preferable to gold or honey. Typically, the proverbial saying of this verse does not state how much better, or in what way better; just "more desired," more coveted, more treasured, more to be pursued.

The Torah is the sum of the triad of steadfast love, justice, and righteousness; "gold" is the quick summary of the triad of might, wisdom, and wealth. The task of nurturing and socialization is to invite sustained critical reflection on choosing one or the other, amid a tradition of those who have been making that choice forever, sometimes toward death and sometimes toward life.

V.

I finish with three conclusions:

1. I am in agreement (only this once) with the great US theologian, Donald Rumsfeld. The Secretary of Defense once famously quipped that there are knowns and there are unknowns. And of the unknowns, there are known unknowns and unknown unknowns. The comment is wiser than it sounds, and one may wish that Rumsfeld had taken the unknown unknowns more seriously. I have been expositing two kinds of wisdom, the fast known wisdom of might, wisdom, and wealth that ends in control; and the slow, unknown mystery of God that opens reality out beyond our control, and requires a relational integrity that appears as steadfast love, justice, and righteousness. Education is the disputatious process of reflection on these two wisdoms.

2. I have offered a list of contrasts and complements that might be supplemented by other pairs of terms concerning *slow* and *fast* wisdom: body/abstraction, neighborhood/club, tradition/syllabus or memo, pain/numbness, dream/possession, vocation/career, imagination/explanation, Torah/gold. It occurred to me that these word pairs boil down to the possibility of committed relationships of integrity in the neighborhood that make for the common good, *vis-à-vis* a mode of life that is indifferent or hostile to the common good.[13] Further, it occurred to me that the relational, covenantal narrative is exactly what we might best learn in kindergarten.[14] How mind-boggling to entertain the thought that what belongs

13 See Walter Brueggemann, *Journey to the Common Good* (Louisville: Westminster John Knox Press, 2010).

14 See Robert Fulghum, *All I Really Need to Know I Learned in Kindergarten* (New York: Villard Books, 1990).

properly to kindergarten continues to belong properly to the work of a serious university—namely, to sustain and evoke relational identity for the sake of the common good.

3. The poetry of Jeremiah strikes me as profoundly contemporary among us; for our time, as that of the ancient city, is very short. We, like that ancient city, are now an anxious society in which "everyone is greedy for unjust gain." We are now a society against which comes an enduring nation whose language we do not know. And we, like that ancient city, are now a society deeply at risk. The poetic response to that risky circumstance seems to me completely pertinent now as then:

> Do not let the wise boast in their wisdom, do not let the mighty boast in their might, do not let the wealthy boast in their wealth; but let those who boast boast in this, that they understand and know me, that I am the Lord; I act with steadfast love, justice, and righteousness in the earth, for in these things I delight, says the Lord. (Jer. 9:23–24)

Contributors

Walter Brueggemann is William Marcellus McPheeters Professor Emeritus of Old Testament at Columbia Theological Seminary. One of the world's leading interpreters of the Old Testament, he is a past president of the Society of Biblical Literature and author of more than one hundred books, including his most recent commentary on Psalms (with W.H. Bellinger, Jr.; Cambridge University Press, 2014) and *A Gospel of Hope* (Westminster John Knox, 2018).

Darin H. Davis is the vice president for university mission at Baylor University. In addition, he serves as director of the Institute for Faith and Learning, holds a faculty appointment in Baylor's Honors Program, and is affiliated faculty in the Department of Philosophy and Baylor's George W. Truett Theological Seminary. His current research focuses on wisdom, friendship, and higher education.

Celia Deane-Drummond is professor of theology at the University of Notre Dame, a position she began after serving as professorial chair in theology and the biological sciences at the University of Chester. A fellow of the Eck Institute for Global Health and the director of the Center for Theology, Science & Human Flourishing at Notre Dame, her books include *The Wisdom of the Liminal: Evolution and Other Animals in Human Becoming* (Eerdmans, 2014) and *Genetics and Christian Ethics* (Cambridge University Press, 2006).

Andrew Delbanco is the Alexander Hamilton Professor of American Studies at Columbia University and serves as the president of the Teagle Foundation. He is the author of *College: What it Was, Is, and Should Be* (Princeton University Press, 2012), and *The Abolitionist Imagination* (Harvard University Press, 2012). He was awarded the 2011 National Humanities Medal by President Barack Obama.

John Haldane is J. Newton Rayzor, Sr., Distinguished Professor in Philosophy at Baylor University. Most recently he has been professor of philosophy at St Andrews University and director of the Centre for Ethics, Philosophy and Public Affairs. He is a Fellow of the Royal Society of Edinburgh, Fellow of the Royal Society of Arts, and Chairman of the Royal Institute of Philosophy. The author of more than 200 academic papers in history of philosophy, philosophy of the mind, metaphysics, and moral and social philosophy, he was appointed by Pope Benedict XVI as a Consultor to the Pontifical Council for Culture in 2005. He is also a member of the Pontifical Academy of Thomas Aquinas.

David Lyle Jeffrey is Distinguished Professor of Literature and the Humanities in the Honors College and Senior Fellow in the Institute for Studies of Religion at Baylor University. A medievalist and scholar of biblical tradition in Western literature and art, his most recent books include *In the Beauty of Holiness: Art and the Bible in Western Culture* (Eerdmans, 2017), *Luke: A Theological Commentary* (Brazos Press, 2012), and *Christianity and Literature: Philosophical Foundations and Critical Practice* (IVP, 2011).

Anthony T. Kronman is Sterling Professor of Law at Yale Law School. A former dean of Yale Law School (1994–2004), he is the author of several books, including *Education's End: Why Our Colleges and Universities Have Given Up on the Meaning of Life* (Yale University Press, 2007), *Democratic Vistas* (ed. with Jedediah Purdy and Cynthia Farrar; Yale University Press, 2004), and *The Lost Lawyer* (Harvard, Belknap Press, 1993).

Index of Names

Index of Subjects